Leaders Praise *The Power of Having Desire*

"For years, I have been drawing cartoons expressing the joy of family life filled with faith, hope, and love. This book is a masterful treatment of those values, and it is packed with similar upbeat entertainment."

—Bil Keane, Creator of *The Family Circus*

"Bruce Garrabrandt is right! A passion, sincerity of purpose, good old-fashioned hard work, and the ability to survive disappointments are the true genesis of creativity and accomplishment. *The Power of Having Desire* reveals an important truth: You are the ultimate architect of your own destiny."

**—Dr. Laura Schlessinger,
Internationally Syndicated Radio Host and Bestselling Author**

"Bruce Garrabrandt has done us all a favor by providing us with the book, *The Power of Having Desire*. This is a humorous, yet deeply analytical look at the potential that is found in each of us. He uses his own experiences as well as those of others to drive that point home in a very entertaining fashion. This is not only interesting reading, but it is quite uplifting."

**—Benjamin S. Carson, Sr., M.D.,
Professor and Director of Pediatric Neurosurgery, Johns Hopkins
Children's Center and Author of *Gifted Hands* and *Think BIG***

"Bruce, you are right about our being at an advantage if we save a spot in our makeup for *youth*. As for myself, I think and act somewhere around the age of 3 years."

—Tim Conway, Comedian

The
POWER
Of
HAVING
DESIRE

The Key Secret to Accomplishing Anything You Really Want

Bruce S. Garrabrandt

A Possibility Press Book

THE
POWER
OF
HAVING
DESIRE

Bruce S. Garrabrandt

Copyright © 2004 by Bruce S. Garrabrandt
ISBN 0-938716-47-6

Published by
Possibility Press

Manufactured in the United States of America

Dedication

For my parents, Doris Horner Garrabrandt
and James Bills Garrabrandt. Through the example
of their lives they taught me the
elements of success.

Contents

Your desire is your most precious gift

Desire Is a Most Priceless Gift

"Desire is the starting point of all achievement. Keep this constantly in mind. Weak desires bring weak results, just as a small amount of fire makes a small amount of heat."
— Napolean Hill —

As a professional artist, I've exhibited my work in more than 200 juried shows over the past 15 years. Many people ask me, "Where did you go to art school?" I tell them I didn't. At the University of Delaware, I studied "pre-unemployment"—I was an English major.

I started drawing as a kid. Creating artwork good enough to frame and hang without embarrassment was a goal I longed to achieve. Mom and Dad kept me well-stocked in paper and pencils. So I got started and, over time, taught myself to draw. When I tell this to people at art shows or seminars, they usually respond by saying, "Oh no, you have a gift. You were born with this talent." I smile and thank them, but I'm thinking, "Yes, I was born with this talent...after a gestation period of about 10,000 hours!"

In teaching myself to draw, I learned something more important than just how to be an artist. I discovered the truth about success. I once looked at successful people and saw only the success. "They were lucky," I'd say to myself. "They were at the right place at the right time. They probably knew somebody or were born into wealth."

What most people don't see when they look at the successful, however, are the countless disappointments and inevitable failures and frustrations encountered along the way. Many believe successful people are lucky or radically different from everyone else. But it's just a convenient way to justify a lack of accomplishment in a particular area in which they would like to succeed. It's often a defensive stance or perhaps an excuse. But it's simply not true.

Let's face it, some people are lazy. It's easier to do just enough to get by—or maybe a little bit more. The path of mediocrity is always crowded. You'll certainly never be lonely there, but neither will you ever be truly successful.

Those who make it big understand that we're all born with great potential. But without having desire we won't amount to much. Nothing is more powerful than someone with a strong sense of purpose and a passionate desire. He or she acts and stays focused on that desire—through all the frustrations, setbacks, and discouragements—until that desire is finally achieved.

Only *You* Can Change Your Life

To accomplish much of anything, you need to integrate these five elements into your daily life:

- Belief in Yourself
- A Sense of Purpose
- Action
- Discipline
- Perseverance

The Power of Having Desire can best be described as a motivational seminar in book form. An artist friend of mine who once held a corporate job told me he sat through a lot of such talks. "The speaker always fires you up," he said, "filling you with enthusiasm. When the talk is over, you leave the room feeling like you could conquer the world. Then you exit the building.... But if you don't take action before the week is over, you're back to your old routine."

 Motivational seminars and books can't change your life. Only *you* can change your life. You need to take the excitement you feel and what you learn and couple it with the power of having desire. Motivational speakers and authors do all the talking and writing, but *you* need to do all the work. The great thing is—you're the one who will get the rewards for doing so.

We may look for shortcuts to the good life. "Someday when I win the lottery…," we may say. Forget it. You have a better chance of being struck by lightning while wearing a chicken suit than you do of winning the lottery.

You are your winning lottery ticket. "The whole secret of a successful life," said Henry Ford, "is to find out what it is one's destiny to do, and then do it." That may sound trite, but it's true. Truth is basic stuff. It has to be so that everyone can understand and profit from it. Do you believe we were created only to have our purpose here be so obscure that only a few people could ever figure it out?

We're on this planet to unlock our potential as human beings—to develop our passions and desires into talents and abilities. That takes dedication and hard (and smart) work. Nothing worthwhile comes otherwise. The only time you can expect quick progress is when your parachute doesn't open.

We Are All Gifted—*The Gift Is Called Desire*

I tell people, "It took me 10,000 hours to learn how to draw." One nice woman said to me, "I could spend 10,000 hours drawing, but my pictures wouldn't look like yours. I'm not gifted like you are." Maybe not. Perhaps it would take her 15,000 or 20,000 hours to learn to draw—or maybe only 5,000 hours. The truth is, she'll never know. The *desire* to draw isn't her gift. If it were, she'd be drawing and investing whatever time was necessary to learn the craft.

I can listen to a classical violinist play beautiful music, and say to myself, "It would be wonderful to play like that." But I will never play, because I lack the desire to practice and learn. The passion needed to dedicate myself to the instrument simply isn't in me. Had I invested as much time playing the violin as I have invested in drawing over the past 36 years—with the same degree of passion—I could be performing in Carnegie Hall today. But the desire to play the violin simply wasn't my gift.

As a teenager, though, whenever I walked through an art museum and saw paintings that moved me, I felt a hunger to learn how that art was created. I studied the techniques—the use of color and light—and got excited by the prospects of improving my own work. I was filled with the *desire* to draw. That desire was and is my gift.

I remember sitting in the second grade, watching the teacher create colored chalk drawings on the blackboard to celebrate the change of seasons. We students were amazed to see these beautiful drawings appear before our eyes, but I wonder how many felt a passion to create their *own* drawings? How many said to themselves, "Whatever it takes, I will learn to do this"? At least one kid was thinking that—*me*.

All of us are born with and can develop desires. Dedicate yourself to yours and you can make them a reality. You can build them into a rewarding life.

Throughout this book I refer to the subject of art, and introduce you to a number of professional artists. Since creating artwork is how I earn my living, this is my primary frame of reference. But *The Power of Having Desire* is not a narrowly focused, "how to" book for aspiring visual artists. Whether you ever want to draw or not is not the issue. The issue is *your* desire—one of your most precious gifts

In the following chapters, information about art is given because the lessons artists striving for excellence learn can be applied to *any* professional or personal endeavor.

Webster's New World Dictionary defines artist as: "(1) a person skilled in any of the fine arts; (2) a person who does anything very well, with imagination and a feeling for form, effect, etc." This second definition is the core of *The Power of Having Desire* and it will define *you*—when you choose to apply the five key elements of success to your own life.

Set No Limits

A powerful fact of life is that your accomplishments can be much greater than you may now envision. Charles Kettering, founder of General Motors, said, "It is amazing what ordinary people can do if they set out without preconceived notions."

Everyone is ordinary, but some of us do extraordinary things, that's all. Unfortunately, most of us grossly undervalue our potential. "But I'm only *one* person," we may say.

Teresa, an artist friend, creates primitive folk art. I love her response to anyone who complains, "But I'm only one person." "Oh really?" she says. "Well, how many people was Thomas Jefferson? How about Eleanor Roosevelt? And what about Mother Teresa?"

"But I'm only one person" is just a convenient excuse for doing nothing, and is best refuted in the biography section of any library. Each of us has unique contributions to make. No matter what our circumstances may be, we're capable of growing into the person we were meant to be. All we need is to have desire.

That's what this book is all about—having *desire*. No one is trapped in some clear polymer—like a seahorse in a paperweight. We *can* better ourselves. Every day we *could* see the awakening of more of our potential. But most of us just sleepwalk through life. Scratch the surface of some people and you find only more surface! In many cases, people are just getting by and melding into the unhappy masses. If, according to the familiar saying, "All the world's a stage," too many of us are content to play the part of the audience. Remember, life is not a spectator sport. So get in the game. Follow your heart's desires and make your dreams come true.

Keep in mind what a wise man said: "Lives of the great men [and women] all remind us that we can make our lives sublime. And in departing, leave behind us footprints on the sands of time."

Life serves us a wonderful hot fudge sundae, but few people come anywhere near to finishing it. Most never get beyond the whipped-cream topping, while some spend their time searching for a napkin to polish the spoon.

The Power of Having Desire is designed to help you enjoy more of your sundae. Now is the time to "dig in" and commit to your desire.

"You can never hit your head against the ceiling of your potential."

—Bruce Garrabrandt

Chapter 1

Believe in Yourself

*"Few of us do more than care for the surface
of our lives. Like thin strips of sod laid over hard clay,
we seldom take root and grow deeply."*
— Bruce Garrabrandt —

S uppose I asked you to sum up, in one sentence, your personal philosophy of life. Could you do it? What would you say? Well, let me give you mine: No matter what you've accomplished in life, you are still mostly potential. Successful people know this. They feel it in their bones. Many have said it better than I can.

Admiral Richard E. Byrd, the polar explorer, believed that "few men or women during their lifetime come anywhere near exhausting the resources dwelling within them. There are deep wells of strength that are never used."

A hundred years ago, psychologist William James said this, "Compared to what we could be, many of us are only half awake."

I also like this bit of wisdom from French writer André Gide: "There are admirable potentialities in every human being. Believe in your own strength. Learn to repeat endlessly to yourself: 'It all depends on me.'"

13

The potential you need to be successful is right inside your heart and mind. Within you lies the power to become the person you want to be—unless, of course, you want to be someone else, that is.

That's the power and the wonder of life. You have, between your ears and in your heart, what it takes to be successful at whatever you want to do. The foundation for your success begins with your heartfelt desire and intention—not so-called gifts and talents. From that you can springboard to build a successful life, whatever that is for you.

Do you recognize these statements?

"Know thyself."

"If you have faith, as a mustard seed, nothing shall be impossible to you."

"Neglect not the gift that is in thee."

You Were Born to Succeed

When life asks us to audition and says, "Show us what you can do," we may manage to position ourselves both on stage and in the audience. In all too many cases, a timid performer stands in the spotlight only to be shouted down by our heckling self seated in the front row.

"No life has ever been lived," said Mark Twain, "which was not a failure in the secret judgment of the person who lived it." People often tend to see themselves, deep down, as damaged goods, fit only for the discount bin of life. Most of us criticize and undervalue ourselves in ways our worst enemies would never dream of. If others saw us as many of us see ourselves, their criticisms would keep us by ourselves, indoors, with the shades pulled down.

Not many people would choose themselves for a best friend. How sad is that? You're all you've got for a lifetime. No matter where you go, you take yourself along for the ride. So you might as well be your best self!

Two elderly women walked into my booth at a recent art show. They struck up a conversation with me about creativity.

"I have no talents," one commented.

"Oh, I'm sure you do," I said.

"No," she insisted, "I can't do anything well."

"How have you survived this long?" I asked playfully.

"I don't know," she laughed.

"Before you leave my booth, would you tell me three qualities you like about yourself?" I asked.

She paused for a moment and said, "I don't know. I've never thought about that." She then turned to her friend and asked, "What do I like about myself?"

"No fair asking someone else," I said. "I want to hear *your* answers."

"Well," she said with a smile, "let me walk around the show, and I'll stop back with my answers."

She never returned.

Surveys have shown that 85 percent of us say we believe in God, yet too few people choose to believe in themselves. To my mind, that's like praising an architect and then being afraid to walk inside one of his or her buildings! We need to be appreciative of our own and others' personal potential. Each of us was born for a reason. *What is my reason ?*

"What lies behind us and what lies before us are tiny matters," wrote Emerson, "compared to what lies within us." You have a vast reservoir of power available to you. Look no further than yourself to find it. That's part of what having faith is all about. You need to trust and know that you were born to live a meaningful life. Do you? If not, would you be willing to?

Your Thoughts Create Your Feelings

The human brain is a source of incredible power for each of us. Someone once said, "As a man thinketh, so is he." What you think determines the way you feel and act. You can do nothing without first thinking about it. If you only rock back and forth, and stare into the middle distance, even these simple actions first require thought.

People are creatures of habit. We establish routines for ourselves. Admittedly, routine is comfortable and gives our lives a sense of order. Look at the daily rituals of your life and examine the patterns of thinking you've formed. Routine actions are the products of such thoughts, and these thoughts and actions create how you view yourself.

Do you see yourself as inadequate? Listen to the messages you give yourself. Begin to observe how your thoughts keep you from venturing beyond what is safe and familiar. The very act of recognizing negative thoughts enables you to gain control over them. Do you ever say to yourself...

"I'm set in my ways"?
"I'm too old to change"?
"I can't do that"?
"I will fail"? or
"It won't work"?

If so, do you understand how saying these things could be hindering your success?

These routine thought patterns are formed to keep our lives predictable and safe—safe, but probably sorry. Our doubts and disclaimers are the silk we spin into protective cocoons. They help avoid facing the risks and responsibilities of change but also keep us from ever having the rewards.

Your thinking determines the degree to which you will fulfill your potential. The great news is that your mind is infinitely more powerful than any negative thoughts to which it may be exposed.

We're often guided by emotions, yet may fail to see that every feeling is brought on by a thought. People frequently take the opposite view: "I feel inadequate, so I don't think I can succeed." But feelings don't dictate thoughts. Thoughts come first and trigger our feelings. Think you are inadequate and a feeling of inadequacy will follow on the heels of that negative thought. In any dance with negativity, your thoughts always lead.

Unleash the Power of Having Desire

My home is 150 years old, built by a prosperous farmer named Samuel Watts. He erected the house as much for his grandchildren as he did for himself. Most people weren't as mobile in those days. Often they were born, lived, and died in the same house, so homes were built to last. In our basement are large, wooden joists which span the width of the house, providing strong structural support. Their function is vital to the integrity and survival of the dwelling.

Recognize the reality of that same kind of support inside yourself. You are created with strong joists which provide the material strength to weather life's disappointments and set-backs. Right thinking unleashes their power. Have faith that they're part of your internal structure.

Believe in yourself. Know that you're made to meet and conquer any challenge or obstacle. You're built for success, and you need to remain aware of your strong joists. Know them firmly in your mind, feel them strongly in your heart, and *nothing* can stop you.

Let's be honest about life. Many ask where we came from and why we're here. We know the people we love will die—including ourselves—and seemingly all too soon. Life is short, so let's make the most of it. No wonder many of us are so insecure and unsure of ourselves—but we needn't be.

Have a trusting attitude. Believe your life is full of purpose and that you possess enormous, untapped potential. Know your life can become rich with meaning and that you are contributing to some greater good. Believe you can become prosperous in the process.

You were born with the freedom of choice. You can be fearful and unsure, or you can choose to be successful and fulfilled. It's all a matter of faith. Your land of possibilities is wide open unless you bring along the fencings and a post-hole digger to fence yourself in.

You may recognize this statement: "Faith is the substance of things hoped for, the evidence of things not seen." Faith is virtually everything. With faith in yourself, each day becomes an adventure as you continue stretching, growing, and experiencing new things.

Have faith and trust that you were designed to play a positive role in the world—that you're here to succeed. You cannot become a success without the love and support of yourself.

Few people commit to themselves and their desire. Most only cohabitate with themselves. Some even act as if they'd prefer a separation from themselves!

When we commit to ourselves and our desire—with faith— we gain an inner peace which accompanies us on our journey. Though we may encounter rocky periods of disappointment and failure along the way, this feeling of serenity will help to smooth our road and keep us moving forward at a steady, confident pace.

We all know people who, even in times of great pressure and stress, somehow manage to maintain an unruffled attitude. Chaos swirls around them in the form of unforeseen challenges, irate customers, clients, or coworkers, phones ringing constantly, and impossible deadlines. Yet these people appear to be the calm in the center of the storm.

"Quiet minds cannot be perplexed or frightened," said Robert Louis Stevenson, "but go on in fortune or misfortune at their own private pace, like a clock ticking during a thunderstorm." Just reading that gives you a peaceful feeling, doesn't it?

Sometimes life dares us to find meaning in our existence. This is when our faith is truly defined. People of faith possess the will to carry on when everything looks bleak. They trust that they are alive for a purpose.

Recognize that you come equipped with sturdy, internal joists. The strength they provide is a fact beyond dispute. People of courage are, and always have been, people of faith. They believe themselves to be part of something richer and deeper than themselves. Remember, as someone said, "As a man thinketh, so is he."

The Miracle of You

We may often fail to appreciate how miraculous life is because we're right smack in the middle of it. The fact is: You are miraculous! Your life is special. Anthropologist Margaret Mead said, "You are unique—just like everyone else." Perhaps her point was to caution us not to let our egos inflate. However, I prefer to interpret her words as a statement about the marvelous nature of human beings. Each of us is endowed with a unique gift called desire and the potential to be an instrument for greater good. Believe this and make personal development a part of the mission of your life.

Personal development and being the best we can be is our job here. Some of us get to the job early and stay late. Some live for vacations and personal days. Others seem to be always on break or out to lunch.

The dawn of each new day needs to be in all our hearts, as well as on the horizon. What skills can we develop to help us best serve others? "To be of use in the world," said Hans Christian Andersen, "is the only way to happiness."

Many people say to me, "But I'm not good at anything. I wasn't born with any talent." Well, no one I know of was born with anything but a talent for crying and creating dirty diapers. To become really good at anything else, you need to work at it. Few people are born with fully formed, innate abilities, but everyone is born with an innate potential that can only be cultivated by desire. To be successful at anything in life, you need to believe this.

① Mentally embrace the power of positive knowing. Begin with a commitment to the fact that you're here to be a creative, productive, successful human being. Accept that everyone has periods of self-doubt, when positive thinking may feel like a meaningless exercise. What sustains you at such times is the underlying knowledge that, despite inevitable failures (which indicate only that you are in training), you're destined to triumph through desire, persistent effort, imagination, and dedication to personal growth. Know this truth—at the core of your being—and successful living will become your reality.

Perhaps your parents failed to inspire you or didn't give proper guidance. Maybe none of your teachers believed in you enough to challenge and motivate you to reach greater heights, perhaps resulting in school years that may have been boring for you. Well, there must be some worthwhile reason that your heart keeps beating and your brain keeps working, or you wouldn't be here. When you accept, with gratitude, the gift of your life and your innate potential, that is reason enough to dedicate yourself to excellence. Your best defense against defeat is gratitude in the present moment. If you still have a pulse—be grateful—you are full of potential.

We were not created with a predestination to fail. We were designed to handle stumbles and falls with the ability to regain our balance, stand up again, and move forward. You learned this a long time ago, or you'd still be crawling around on the floor on your hands and knees. What you discovered when you were a toddler is a lesson to be carried throughout life. It's okay to fall down now and then, but you were built to stand up and get to wherever you wanted to go. Your creative possibilities become virtually infinite once you recognize your potential.

Are you nearsighted to the majesty whirling around you? As you acquire a broader view, you can expand your life and enrich its meaning. We are given both the power to reason and the power to believe. Logic and faith are mighty tools. The challenge may be to discern when to use each.

If you feel yourself drowning in a seemingly meaningless life, just clinging to reason cannot save you. Only by letting go—which is an act of faith—will you find yourself floating, buoyed up by an inner confidence and calm, toward a bountiful shore. Philosopher John Stuart Mill said, "One person with belief is equal to a force of 99 who have only interests." Frank Lloyd Wright, the great architect, told us, "The thing always happens that you believe in, and the belief in a thing makes it happen."

We're here to dream & to do,

To believe that you have been given no gifts is to say you were created without purpose. I cannot accept that. How about you? Each of us is gifted with desires and interests and the ability to choose that course of action which we believe will develop us.

Turn inward. See the miracle that you are and recognize your current and potential strengths. Set a goal that'll help you best utilize your desire and begin taking steps toward achieving it. Think. Plan. Act. We're here to dream and do. You've been put on this earth for a reason. Whether or not you choose to determine what it is and focus on it is another matter.

If you're not currently a self-starter, then you need to become one. Life will rarely leave you feeling burned out once you learn how to light your own fire and keep it roaring. It's your responsibility to pursue excellence—no one can do it for you. You owe it to yourself, your family, and your fellow human beings to be the best you can be.

Potential was given to you at birth and the supporting structure is in place. Know that a great power lies within you. You are your own safety net. Have faith in yourself. "As soon as you trust yourself," said the poet, Goethe, "you will know how to live."

Follow the Dream in Your Heart

When Walt Disney first made the rounds in Hollywood, peddling his concept of a talking mouse as being a "movie star," studio executives dismissed it as far-fetched and unworkable. They wouldn't take the idea seriously.

Undaunted, young Disney took it upon himself to create and market this dream of his called "Mickey." It was no small effort to succeed. But he refused to let the negative opinions of others undermine his confidence. Walt Disney believed in himself. The results of his unshakable optimism survive and thrive, stronger than ever, more than 35 years after his death.

Whenever he got a new idea, Disney said, he asked 20 people what they thought of it. If they were unanimous in their disapproval, he'd go full speed ahead with it. Disney showed us how faith and trust can make lasting power. When you follow your dream, whatever it is, it'll take you wherever you're supposed to go. You can count on it.

Your potential is a vast, perhaps unexplored, continent. Be courageous and venture into it. If you foolishly choose to ignore a large part of your potential, you won't accomplish what was in your heart and on your mind to do. Be strong and take action. Your potential is yours to claim. Have and develop the desire, faith, and optimism to go for it.

You Create Your Own World

In a real sense, you create your own world. If you see it through cynical eyes, your life can become a pointless struggle—a predatory affair in which narrow, selfish motives direct human behavior, and strangers are viewed with suspicion.

But when you see the world through the eyes of a successful person, it becomes a wonderful place where the loving gift of desire has been cultivated. You will find countless examples of warm, friendly people whose conduct enriches the lives of others, whose desires ennoble and dignify all of us. People with a desire perspective create a world of purpose and deep meaning. For them, life becomes a beautiful adventure, a precious opportunity to develop and express their gifts and abilities in positive, fulfilling ways.

Cruel and brutal, or loving and generous, the kind of world you see will determine the quality of people and experiences which fill your life. In either case, your expectations will be fulfilled.

Stop Comparing Yourself to Others

A man looked at my drawings at a recent art show and said, "You certainly were given a gift—a wonderful talent."

"Thank you," I said, "but the gift wasn't talent. It was the *desire* to draw. I'm self-taught."

"I think you have to possess the talent to begin with," he told me. "A kid I was friends with in grade school used to make drawings of buildings. They were quite beautiful. I was jealous because it came so easily to him. I couldn't possibly draw as well as he did. I tried, but it was frustrating for me, so I gave up. Now I just admire other artists' works and hang them on my walls. Today, my artist friend is a successful architect. Others could study and practice forever and never come close to being as good an architect as he is. No matter what they do, they'll always be average."

"Maybe so," I told him, "but we're not here to become the best that someone else can be. We need to grow into the best that *we* can be."

Now, you could say to me, "That sounds very nice, but not everyone can be great." But you'd be wrong. We are all born with the seed of greatness which simply needs to be nurtured. You may never become famous, but you can become great. All "fame" means is that more people know about your greatness. I may never be a famous artist, but I'm inspired by the Great Masters. I marvel at the work of colored pencil artists whose productivity and recognition outdistance mine. So what? I love to draw, and I've persevered long enough to become somewhat accomplished. As Mother Teresa said, "It's not how much we do, but how much love we do it with."

Having developed a degree of expertise in my field, I'm able to live quite well by doing what I enjoy. That, in my mind, is success. I don't have to be the most well known, compared to other artists, at what I do. And you don't need to compare yourself to others in your field either. We long to soar like eagles, forgetting that sparrows, too, can fly. They are being the best they can be.

You and I can be better than we are. There's always room for growth. Someone once said, "There is no ceiling on effort." What an exciting fact of life! You can continue the joy of overcoming challenges by using your desire to develop talents, gifts, and skills—for the rest of your life.

Successful people face obstacles just like everyone else—and more. They're growing and stretching, rather than settling for less as average people do. They simply choose to deal with and overcome their challenges with desire in a positive, possibility thinking way. Adversity, like a strong competitor when met and dealt with, can bring unexpected abilities out of us which can be astonishing. The obstacles you overcome are like chisels which slowly sculpt you into a work of art.

Admire other people's levels of accomplishment, but don't be intimidated or awed by them. Otherwise, you may rob yourself of the opportunity to become more than you ever dreamed possible. Remember, there's always someone who has more than you do. Rather than comparing ourselves to others, we need to be comparing what and where we are now to what and where we could be.

Remember those kids in high school who never had to study? (You may have been one of them!) Good grades seemed to come effortlessly. More than once I sat sweating over essay test questions while the student next to me had already turned in his or her blue (test) book. I, in no way, could have competed with that student's speed of learning and recall. So what? Would it have been better had I torn up my test book and left the classroom? If learning a subject takes you five times longer than it does for someone else, so what? As long as you eventually master the material and keep moving forward, isn't that what matters most?

I once knew a man, we'll call him Fred, who continually compared himself to others. He was caught in the comparison trap. Fred measured his success strictly in material terms. He liked to view himself as doing better and having more than those around him. It wasn't enough for Fred that he owned a nice house. The fact that most of his friends still lived in apartments and condos is what made the house special to him. His appreciation for what he owned was always predicated on how it stacked up against what others possessed. That determined his level of satisfaction. He involved himself in a constant, unrelenting game of one-upmanship.

On several occasions, Fred talked about an elderly relative. When this person died, he would inherit his big old house in the mountains. Rather than enjoying his current home, Fred and his wife mentally had this man dead and buried and were talking about what they'd do with the place. They were practically picking out furniture and choosing curtains.

How unfortunate it was that Fred based his happiness on what he owned and obsessed over how his things ranked with others' possessions. He'll be forever running a race he cannot win, scrambling in vain to catch up to people who have more.

Rather than living in competition with friends, neighbors, associates, and coworkers, Fred—and those like him—would do well to step back and look with heartfelt gratitude upon their most valuable possession: the gift of life itself. Instead of concerning ourselves with how well *others* are doing, we all need to be grateful for what we have and ask ourselves, "How can I become a better person?" As a by-product of our growth and contribution, we'll be able to enjoy the fruits of our labor.

Life offers so much more to those who drop out of the "rat race" and find the value in each moment. When we compete with ourselves through personal growth—and strive to realize more of our inner capabilities—we discover how little time remains for competition with anyone else.

Rediscover Your Sense of Wonder

"It takes a long time to become young," said Pablo Picasso. He understood well how the root of our creativity is founded in our sense of wonder.

"What do you want to be when you grow up?" adults asked us when we were kids. "As powerful as I am now," could have been our answer. Young children are full of creative power. Their imaginations are rich with fanciful ideas and the desire to play and learn. Unfortunately, those qualities are often squelched during our school years by adults who claim they know better.

Robert Fulghum, bestselling author of *All I Really Need To Know I Learned In Kindergarten*, is often invited to speak at schools, usually to kindergarten and college-level classes. He is always struck by the difference in self-confidence between the two groups.

For example, Fulghum asks a roomful of five-year-olds, "How many of you can sing?" All hands go up. He asks, "How many of you can draw?" Everyone can draw. "How many can dance?" They all can. "How many can act?" All hands wave eagerly.

Fulghum also asks these same questions when speaking to college students. Unfortunately, he sees relatively few hands raised in positive response, and those who *do* respond are usually timid about it.

Fulghum wonders what happened to the desire and boundless enthusiasm of these former five-year-olds. Sadly, he hears students talk about their limitations, lack of confidence, and circumstances.

Large classrooms of students are generally not conducive to the development of individuality—depending, to some extent, of course, on the teacher or professor. Following instructions and learning by rote are usually emphasized over creativity and imaginative play. Reading, writing, and arithmetic are essential elements of a solid education, but they aren't enough for realizing one's potential. Some even say that all they learned in school was how to pass tests.

If we are to understand our unique gift of desire, we need to first reclaim the sense of wonder about life and its marvelous possibilities that we had as children. Such awe stimulates creative thinking which can guide us to greater achievement.

Commitment to keeping your creative spirit alive provides you with opportunities daily to experience, once again, all the magic of childhood—this time without getting chicken pox.

Those who seem to be stuck in the same old monotonous routines have made their minds virtual monuments—their lives reflecting regimented, boring patterns of thinking. Those who are excited about life and constantly exploring and testing their potential have made their minds jungle gyms for their imagination. How about you?

One Father's Legacy

When children have someone nurturing their sense of wonder, it can have a powerful, positive effect that sets them up for a life of accomplishment.

While a student at the University of Delaware, I made regular pilgrimages to the Brandywine River Museum in Chadds Ford, Pennsylvania. There I found inspiration in the work of America's foremost artistic family—the Wyeths. N.C. Wyeth was celebrated for his illustrations of literary classics. But his greatest artistic achievement was the desire for creative spirit that he imparted to his children.

A Smithsonian program for public television profiled the Wyeth family. Interviews with N.C.'s children, by then senior citizens, revealed the profound impact their father's childlike approach to life had had on them.

Nat, the eldest son, was a successful engineer. He held 23 patents. Among his many inventions was the plastic soda bottle. Nat's sister Ann became an accomplished musician and composer. Siblings Carolyn, Henriette, and Andrew followed in their father's artistic footsteps.

Now, some may say all this talent was in their genes. But don't you believe it. What made the difference in their lives was how N.C. taught his children to observe their world. He understood that life only exhilarates those who take big, spontaneous gulps of it.

"Soak it all up," he advised them. "Be like a sponge." He was determined to infuse his children with a lifelong creative spirit and sense of wonder, and he certainly succeeded in doing so. Writer David McCullough described it as "growing up in a magical household where being creative and being alive were one and the same thing."

N.C. was a dedicated, compassionate father. He never talked down to his children—he treated them as peers. "Keep alive to everything and carry it with you," he told them. "When you are open to all of life, you're in a schoolroom."

Play was an essential component of the Wyeth household. The family performed elaborate skits and often filmed these amateur productions as home movies. N.C. brought home piles of paper, pencils, and paints for his kids.

"Use plenty of materials," he instructed. "Plenty of paint." The man overflowed with passion for life. He savored it in all of its details. He exposed his children to a world of excellent music, excellent books, and excellent art. He taught them how to see, hear, and think expansively. "Do everything in a big way!" was his fatherly advice.

If we wade through life, we'll be happy only up to our shins. To be drenched with delight, we must live deeply. N.C. Wyeth knew this and lived it every day.

He once took his family to see the film *Mutiny on the Bounty*. When the movie ended, he quickly herded his children into the lobby to observe the audience as these people exited the theater. "Look at all those dull faces," he said. He warned them about the great limitation of film—it offers moviegoers no interaction of imagination. It is a passive endeavor of watching other people live their lives—rather than fully living our own. It's often a temporary escape to alleviate the boredom of the average person's life.

The Smithsonian's biography of the Wyeths concludes with excerpts from one of N.C.'s many letters. The artist's words reflect his personal life philosophy, a great lesson in how to live creatively. We would all do quite well to adopt it for ourselves:

> "My imagination is on fire. The universe towers in my mind a great, overpowering mystery. The significance of the tiniest speck of bark on the pine tree assumes the proportions of the infinite sky. My brain almost bursts with the effort to really appreciate the meaning of life, of existence. I ardently promise, with all my soul, to do my best to make my short life of use, to add an infinitesimal light to the world."

Creative vision isn't a matter of having the right genetics. It comes to us when we rediscover that five-year-old child within ourselves, and proclaim to the world, "Yes, I can do that!"

I'm a person of average intelligence, as you may be. That's okay. It doesn't hold me back, and it doesn't need to hold you back either. Why? Even with average intelligence I have more potential than I can possibly realize in my lifetime, and so do you. So grow and expand your horizons as much as you can. Embrace your life's deepest desire and greatest challenge. Creatively be the best you can be, as that's where you'll find your most valuable contribution and greatest joy.

What About Self-Esteem?

I'd love to do away with the term "self-esteem." So many people blame their failures and unhappiness on their poor self-esteem—their lack of respect for themselves. I listen to talk radio when I'm drawing and hear people frequently saying things like this:

> "I grew up in a dysfunctional family. I was never made to feel important. Because of the way I was treated in the past, I don't feel good about myself. I have low self-esteem."

This may well be true, but it shouldn't be held up as a banner you wave hoping for sympathy, or used as an excuse to prevent you from growing and moving on. We all hurt in some ways—we've all had our share of challenges. Don't kid yourself that you're the only one with hurdles to leap over.

Sometimes self-esteem is linked to family history. I especially like Lincoln's opinion of obsession with ancestry: "I'm less concerned with what my grandfather did than in what his grandson will do."

Problems arise if we allow our self-esteem to be dependent upon circumstances outside ourselves. This leaves us totally vulnerable to exterior forces. Take this version of self-esteem and throw it out, along with all the negative messages you may have given yourself. You need self-belief, which no one else can give you. Others can encourage you, but you are the only one with the power to better yourself. It's up to you to desire to create the circumstances you need to live a fulfilling life.

Self-belief is a paycheck earned through rigorous employment of your abilities and potential. Anyone who's waiting for handouts might as well forget it. Handouts don't build self-belief—they reinforce weakness. If you expect others to do your job for you, you're likely to wait forever. You're the one whose job it is to nurture your desire.

Are You Safe and Secure?

In the "Parade of Life," people often settle for being the crepe paper on a poorly constructed float. Don't be one of them.

What do you dream of being or doing? Write a list of any reasons why you think you'll probably never achieve your dream. Then—and this is the important part—throw the list away! Stop making excuses. Life offers us the run of the mansion, but our comfort zone is usually inside the broom closet.

Why aren't most of us vigorously pursuing our dreams? First of all, a lot of people feel safe in their daily routines. They opt for security. They are letting themselves be held hostage by it. But, as General Douglas MacArthur warned, "There is no security—there is only opportunity." And as humorist James Thurber said, "There's no safety in numbers, or in anything else."

If you pause amid the business of your life to seek out one, tiny corner of safety and security, you're only kidding yourself. Don't look for a safety net in life. Your life is an opportunity. It's better not to be safe and sorry. Become a sensible risk-taker. Begin making plans to become greater than you are. If you want more out of life, you need to get more out of yourself. It's a fundamental fact that, as long as you continue to have brain-wave activity, you can do more. You are always unfinished business—a work in progress. Your growth needs to remain number one on your "to do" list. The more you grow, the more you can succeed.

Security yawns and closes its eyes to possibility. The moment you make security your primary goal in life, you begin to die. To settle for comfortable routine is like doing all of your grocery shopping at a convenience store. You'll pay an exorbitant price for what you purchase there. The cost is your precious potential.

Look around you. Most people, perhaps unknowingly, choose to shut down their desires and remain unfulfilled. They conform to the conventional and blend with the herd. Why does Mediocrity sit and scratch itself on Mount Untapped Potential? Because it's easier! We can opt for mediocrity in life and still have our basic needs met. We can get food, shelter, and clothing without pushing ourselves very hard. But is that how you want to live?

Though we're all meant to be in the game, the sidelines are full of people out of uniform, sitting on lawn chairs. "I do enough to get by" seems to be their personal life slogan. Two other mottoes could be "Don't make waves," and "Just go with the flow."

We aren't here to be average. Average is the top of the bottom and the bottom of the top. It's really nowhere. We were created to excel and succeed. In time, "the path of least resistance" often becomes heavily rutted with boredom and dissatisfaction.

The creative spirit of desire is built into us. To ignore it in favor of comfort and conventional routine is to squander the greatest of gifts. Push out of habit and into new, positive directions. Discover more of yourself.

Part of your life's "job description" requires you to take a brain that's gray on the outside and, through all the days of a lifetime, fill it with brightness and color. Suppose your life were suddenly transformed into a box of 64 Crayola crayons. Which colors have had the most use? If you're not fulfilling your dreams, as most people aren't, the black, white, and gray crayons are probably worn down to nubs.

A lifetime commitment to an evolving self is a marriage made in heaven, and heaven-on-earth lies within us as we follow our hearts and pursue our dreams.

"Artists" Are Everywhere

People sometimes look closely at my artwork and say something like, "I'm surprised that you can do this with just pencils and a blank sheet of paper." While a very nice compliment, this implies that artistic expression comes from some secret, powerful place. Believe me, it doesn't.

An artist creates by starting with a blank canvas or paper, but never from a blank mind. Human beings cannot create anything without thought. We build upon what we already know. The more we learn and grow, the more fertile our minds become, and increase the likelihood that imaginative ideas will sprout and flourish. Creativity arises from a mix of our life experiences, what our hearts dictate, what we study, and the unique reworking of that which already exists.

A new drawing is affected by and made, in part, from all the drawings which preceded it. Each work of art is part of an ongoing education; one more step forward in the incremental process called creation. Nothing new is produced whole and unattached—an artistic island—even though it may appear that way.

Artists aren't wizards; yet, because art is a visual manifestation of creativity, its impact on others can be quite dramatic. Step outside the arena, and you can find the same wonderful creativity expressed in countless other ways. Teachers, scientists, chefs, surgeons, secretaries, business owners, computer programmers, and many others demonstrate great artistic abilities—perhaps without realizing it.

Steve was a plumber who did work for my parents many years ago. He once showed me snapshots of an especially challenging plumbing job he'd tackled. The photos pictured a narrow, cramped crawlspace in which he had assembled an innovative line of pipes and ran them up into an old house. Obviously his work required great imagination and skill.

Steve was neither a sophisticated nor articulate man, but he was an artist, nonetheless. I remember his pleasure in showing me those crawlspace photographs. He was beaming. Like Handel completing his "Hallelujah Chorus," or Hemingway finishing a short story, Steve, the plumber, felt that same glow of satisfaction experienced by artists working at their creative best.

One autumn day in Rhinebeck, New York, I saw a long line of people waiting outside a small art gallery. They'd come to see artist Charles Wysocki and to have him autograph their copy of his latest book. Seeing that line of eager people, stretching down the block, reminded me of my father.

For many years, my parents operated a drive-in restaurant, famous locally for its delicious homemade ice cream, which Dad took great joy in making. A small room within the restaurant housed a huge metal vat. Into it Dad poured the richest dairy cream available, along with a variety of flavors he had spent decades perfecting. The results were incomparably delicious.

A line always formed outside the ice cream room whenever Dad finished a batch of his latest frozen masterpiece. Carhops, cooks, and soda jerks stood clutching cups and spoons, waiting to get a taste of it—fresh from the machine. My father's years of hard work and creative experimentation had combined to produce the best ice cream anywhere. Dad, too, was an artist— the Degás of dairy desserts!

Creativity Is Universal

"I admire your artistic ability," people say to me. "I can't draw a straight line."

"If that were true," I tell them, "you never would've learned to print your name."

As kids, we sat hunched over sheets of yellow lined paper, gripping thick pencils, slowly, painstakingly printing each letter of the alphabet. We drew lots of straight lines then, along with some beautiful loops and swirls. Later, we graduated to writing and, after much practice, our work on paper often developed a flowing, seamless quality. Don't tell me your handwriting is terrible. That doesn't matter. The point is you can do it.

Handwriting is a skill you acquired and is, quite literally, your personal, creative signature. The same people who tell me they can't draw a straight line will purchase my work and often sign their credit card with truly distinctive handwriting. Creativity flows from their fingers, but they don't see it!

Creative potential dwells in all of us. It's a universal trait, waiting to be discovered and embraced. But what do some of us 'say to ourselves? "Oh, I don't have a creative bone in my body." Unfortunately, this belief becomes our reality, and a vital part of what it means to be human is lost.

We have a critic in our heads who may delight in analyzing our creative thoughts only to find fault with them. Your critic is the part of you which says "it can't be done" or, "that idea is no good."

W.C. Fields said, "Critics, to be taken seriously, should be able to create as well as criticize." Well, your inner critic cannot create. It can hone, polish, and perfect, but it doesn't produce anything. If it whispers inside your head, "You can't do that," you need to tell your inner critic—in no uncertain terms—to be quiet.

Brainstorming Can Help You Move Ahead

In teaching myself to draw, I discovered, quite by accident, an effective way to quiet my inner critic, when necessary. Sitting with a black and white photograph of comedians Laurel and Hardy and some art paper, I drew a portrait of their faces. The drawing didn't go well. As I struggled to get a likeness, my inner critic kept up his constant progress report. "Those eyes don't look right...That nose is crooked...The mouth is all wrong...." My eraser got a good workout. In frustration I finally turned the photograph upside-down and drew it that way. Suddenly, my inner critic quieted down and I was able to freely draw what I saw. Gone were eyes, nose, and mouth. Now I was just copying curves and lines and various shades of gray. I got lost in my work. Hours later I turned my paper right-side-up to study the results. While nowhere near perfect, my drawing was obviously a portrait of Laurel and Hardy. I was thrilled! Now my inner critic returned and began giving instructions on how to improve the work. This time his criticism was helpful. He guided me to achieve a better likeness.

I learned a valuable lesson that day. Quieting the inner critic was essential if I was going to be an artist and create drawings. By turning photographs upside-down, I could work without critiquing every line I put down on paper. I found drawing an eye to be impossible, but drawing the upside-down shape of an eye came easily. My inner critic could be moved aside long enough for me to get a picture onto paper, and then I could invite him back to look at my work and offer good advice.

Each of us has two, separate "people" inside our heads: child/creator and an adult/critic share the same cranium. Each needs to know his proper place. You are their overseer. Your role in the creative process is to engage each of these two selves at the right time. This comes with practice.

Writers know this. They often use brainstorming to silence the adult/critic and allow the child/creator to play on paper. Thoughts on a given topic are written quickly, as they come to mind, without regard to quality. The point is to fill the page with ideas, to get thoughts onto paper before the critic has a chance to complain about content. Once brainstorming is completed, the critic is welcomed back to organize, edit, and craft the words into a finished work of art.

Better to gather a large volume of information, and imaginatively sift through it, than to begin with an inadequate supply of material and struggle to find creative gold there. You can whittle away from too large a block of wood in a myriad of ways, but your creative options shrink when you're given only a knife and a Popsicle stick.

In any creative endeavor, you hold the power to keep your adult/critic at arm's length long enough to give your child/creator free rein. The process is a skill, not unlike the scrawling of letters onto yellow paper with a fat pencil. With patience, time, and practice, you can learn to bring forth more of your creative potential without sabotaging it.

Your spontaneous child/creator yells "Action!" and lets the creative cameras roll. Judgment, your adult critic, banned from the set during filming, steps in later to edit the footage.

Carry Only the Best for Yourself

To know yourself is your personal challenge. Before you can fully appreciate your potential, you need to take a long, hard, honest look at yourself. The people and events of your life, both past and present, exert powerful influences on you. To understand what truly motivates us requires the confrontation of our inner fears and painful memories, which we all have. Too often though, we allow them to shape our entire approach to living. But, being aware of them can help us put everything into a better perspective.

Recognizing how past criticisms, injustices, and failures influence the way you act—and react—today, is essential for you to break free from old, limiting thoughts. To know yourself is to uncover the truth that you are stronger than your fear. No matter what fears you may have, you are in control. You can take action to overcome them.

You've been walking around inside your own skin your whole life. Tell me, who's in a better position than you to know your personal doubts, fears, and insecurities? Who, but you, has the deepest insight to your dreams and desires? Who is closest to your potential talents and abilities?

Teachers, clergy, counselors, leaders, mentors, and perhaps others can guide you to better understand yourself and your motives, but the decision to act in your best interest always rests with you. Ultimately, you're in control of how you choose to relate to yourself and the world. When you stop to think about it, that's a tremendous amount of power. Stop to think about it…then act on it!

Picture your personal challenges as fitting neatly into a container the size of your head. During your lifetime so far, you have managed to haul that container and all of its garbage around, but feel free to dump the unwanted contents any time you choose. Carry only the best for yourself. Deep down inside you know what you need to do. So commit to memory these words from the Roman statesman, Cicero: "Nobody can give you wiser advice than yourself."

Clichés Can Be Uplifting

Why write a book about the elements of success? Everyone knows them. "Believe in yourself!" "Follow your dream!" "Be disciplined!" "Never give up!" These expressions were clichés long before we walked the planet. We've heard them thousands of times. But have we embraced them, ingested them, and made them a core part of who we are?

Some of us take clichés and personalize them in the form of negative self-talk—giving ourselves thousands of excuses for not achieving our dreams.

We choose to stay where we are by the negative cliché thoughts we hold about ourselves and our circumstances. The excuses we cling to become the steel bars we fashion into a personal prison, a safe little world called "But."

"I would believe in myself, but..."
"I'd like to follow my dream, but..."
"I could be disciplined, but..."
"I wouldn't have given up, but..."

Such clichés may be like warm blankets, tucked all around to keep us safe from those monsters—change, risk, and vulnerability—that lurk under the bed.

We may look at our situations and find so many reasons why our personal circumstances preclude the fulfillment of our dreams. If so, this becomes our reality.

People visiting my booth at arts festivals sometimes say to me, "Oh! I have your artwork." I thank them, but when I ask, "Which pictures do you own?," often they cannot recall the scenes they've bought. Even when my work has been decorating their walls for years, some customers find themselves struggling to remember which framed prints they've purchased.

I laugh when this happens and tell them not to feel bad. I experience the same problem, and I don't think it's because my work is less memorable than that of other artists.

"I like to rotate my pictures," I tell people. "When we change the scenery on our walls, it helps to keep our vision fresh." Day after day, we see the same pictures, until they no longer register on our minds. There the art hangs, in plain view, and yet we seem to look right through it.

What's true for artwork also holds true for clichés. For example, all of us are familiar with the following lines:

"Never put off until tomorrow what you can do today."
"Haste makes waste."
"You can lead a horse to water, but you can't make him drink."
"A fool and his money are soon parted."
"We reap what we sow."

Through the years, we've heard these and other similar clichés so often that they may no longer have much impact on us. That's unfortunate. The reason clichés are so durable is because they usually state truths. The best advice is often the oldest, most basic information we know. Don't take clichés for granted simply because they've been hanging on your mind's wall for a long time. Take time to really see them, hear them, and understand what practical applications they can have in your own life. Use them to your advantage.

Why Would You Want to Act Like a Bird?

When a bird sees its reflection in a windowpane, it often reacts as if the image is another bird about to invade its territory. Its response is then to fly into the glass to attack the "intruder". If the impact causes no injury, the bird may repeat its attack, crashing against the window again and again, to get at that "enemy" bird, until it finally renders itself stunned, injured, or dead. The bird doesn't realize that its injuries are self-inflicted.

We watch this happen and sadly shake our heads. "Poor bird," we may say. Yet, people often engage in similar, self-destructive behavior. We may continually fly into the glass of negative thought patterns which have hurt us in the past. We may crash against the same harmful circumstances many times over, all the while failing to see how we're contributing to our own pain and unhappiness.

Some people are worse to themselves than our feathered friends. Some of us understand the harm we're doing to ourselves, but we keep doing it anyway!

"I've always flown into the glass."

"I know this is hurting me, but what else can I do?"

"I deserve to fly into windowpanes."

"If I fly hard and fast enough, I'll break through this glass."

"You can blame me for crashing against the window, but I didn't put it there."

Maybe it's time for some of us to change our flight patterns.

In performing from the sheet music of our daily lives, we may often repeat the same tune with little variation, no longer hearing the notes we're playing. We think and act in established ways because they feel familiar to us. Though they may bring unhappiness and be detrimental to our personal growth, they're still what we know best. The creature of habit may be slowly curling itself around our creative potential, eventually strangling it.

You may want to think of habit and routine as comfortable old clothes. Though they're frayed and out of style, you continue to wear them. But they do limit the places where you can go. Go ahead and get rid of them so you can move on.

Get Rid of the Trash

Twice a year, our small town has a special trash and cleanup day. Unwanted large appliances and bulky items, which ordinarily couldn't be put out with the weekly garbage, are picked up and taken away.

Wouldn't it be wonderful if people used the same approach to rid their minds of lazy, useless, negative thoughts? Dusty old prejudices; worn out, habitual ways of doing things; and dog-eared opinions need to be dragged outside and deposited at the curb.

I enjoy listening to radio personality, Dr. Laura Schlessinger. "Mother Laura," as she calls herself, is a controversial woman, largely because she holds people accountable for their actions. Her radio program is designed to promote moral behavior. This ethical stance was bound to make her unpopular with some listeners. Playwright Henrik Ibsen said, "Never put on your good trousers to go out fighting for truth and justice."

A scientist by training, Dr. Laura says habits could be more than just familiar patterns of behavior. They may actually become hard-wired into us, by establishing neural pathways in the brain, reinforced every time we engage in specific thoughts or actions.

She believes in "manual override," the power of the human will to overcome unwanted patterns set down in our brains. Dr. Laura used this technique to manage, and ultimately eliminate, her own crippling panic attacks.

"This act of will may be excruciatingly difficult," she says, "but it isn't impossible." Meeting tough challenges in this way, and conquering them, can change your life dramatically. In the face of some difficult task, our *lack* of will can create a glare so bright that we want to hide in the shadows of "impossibility."

You need to rule as a monarch over your kingdom of thought. Sadly, some choose to abdicate their power to other people. If you are one of those people, reclaim your power—it belongs to you!

Keep Your Mental Battery Charged

Every human being comes equipped with a remarkable, permanent mental battery. Failures and setbacks may drain it of a lot of power, but it generally has some energy left. Fortunately, our internal battery is fully rechargeable, provided we attach it to currents of positive thoughts and actions.

It's the supply of optimism that keeps our battery recharging during the rough times. We experience it as a spirited determination to be flexible and adapt if setbacks occur, a willingness to see new opportunity in any failure, and a desire to find whatever resources are needed to move again toward our goals and dreams.

By contrast, any mental battery attached to negativity becomes weakened further in periods of crisis. Acids of cynicism and hopelessness deplete its capacity to rejuvenate. These corrode our batteries and are experienced as withdrawal in the face of obstacles, a refusal to overcome new challenges, and a feeling of being victimized, rather than empowered, in moments of crisis.

People in this deteriorating state often engage in self-destructive behaviors, in an attempt to escape from their problems. Left unchecked, this continual current drain results in a dead battery. Unless these people can get a charge of optimism, they'll find themselves permanently stuck. They're unable to move past their problems with their current level of thinking.

Plug yourself into a positive powerful source now, so you can rejuvenate the energy necessary to sustain you when challenges come. Keep your mental battery charged!

The most powerful, mind-altering "drug" available to you is a positive change of attitude. This attitude change produces a continual feeling of gratitude, the foundation for a happy life. Simply taking a moment to mentally run through what you are grateful for can give you a positive charge.

Your mind possesses incredible power. You picture things mentally daily. Your imagination continually projects thoughts of what you want and expect from life onto your mental movie screen. You can picture anything you desire, so go ahead and create your life as a stirring epic.

Positive Statements Can Help You Overcome and Achieve

It's been said that nothing that happens to you in life is bad, so long as (a) you learn from the experience and (b) you survive it.

Challenges and upheavals are inevitable events in everyone's life. "This, too, shall pass," as Abraham Lincoln said, is a good adage to keep in mind. If we don't do something about it, the stress associated with traumatic experiences can stay with us, affecting our ability to cope with and conquer adversity.

Stress is a part of life. We all need to deal with it. Fortunately, we can control our response to it. Rather than denying the stress—make it work for you. Harness yourself with the right mental attitude.

The Chinese word for crisis consists of two brush strokes. One stroke signifies danger; the other, opportunity. Why not make this part of your personal credo? *A crisis is simply an opportunity.* Have you ever reached a new level in a relationship because of how well you handled the crisis that person presented to you? It simply turned out to be an opportunity to strengthen the relationship.

A positive approach to problems and challenges as opportunities to grow can enhance your health. Scientific research has demonstrated this. Think of your mind as a chemist and your brain as the laboratory. As you think optimistic thoughts, it causes reactions in your brain—releasing chemicals which positively affect your central nervous system, organ function, and immune system's ability to resist disease.

When you focus on positive possibilities in times of setback, your chemist-mind also becomes your personal physician! Crises will actually strengthen you and improve your health— when you choose to cope with them positively and confidently.

Our minds work for us or against us. Have faith that everything will work out if you're faced with the possibility of failure. Consciously adjust your mental attitude to find solutions. As a result, you'll grow stronger and more confident through challenges.

The late Dr. Norman Vincent Peale spent decades instructing people to fill their minds with meaningful, positive statements. Here are just a few for your mental files:

"I can if I think I can."
"Faith can solve any personal problem."
"I was made to handle challenges."

These aren't just simple, pleasant mantras to be tucked away in your memory. Use them, now, to actively establish a positive mental foundation for yourself. As challenges arise, you will stay strong as you work your way through them. When problems and setbacks rattle your life like seismic waves, you won't collapse. You'll remain structurally sound.

As you repeat these positive statements to yourself, feel them working to strengthen you. Remember, you were born with the potential to succeed in every area of your life. Have the faith and reassurance that you're not alone as you deal with challenges, and persist until you handle them successfully.

When you build internal fortitude, challenges serve to stimulate and activate your creative capabilities. You respond to challenges with enthusiasm and a determined spirit. You learn to adapt and advance. Stressful situations can inspire you into productive action when you choose to look at them as opportunities.

Saying, "I can't" cuts you off from the possibilities. You would allow fear to immobilize you. Why do that to yourself? Fortunately, thoughts aren't chiseled into your mind; they're only written in mental chalk. With your will to think positively you can overcome negative patterns. As you practice daily, you can erase and replace them.

You were made to grow and move forward. Your faith, courage, and resourcefulness will help you plot the best course to follow. Your brain was given to you as standard equipment. Faith, courage, and dedication to conquer obstacles are options you need to buy. Your character is the currency. Nothing you do can be out of character for you. What you do demonstrates it. Build yours through a positive response to life's challenges. Be an excellent example for others to follow.

For Dr. Peale, his positive thinking contributed to nearly a century of robust living, learning, and leading. His life is a great testimonial to the effectiveness of positive statements.

Choose Your Words Carefully

Intimidation. Who hasn't been gripped by fear in some moment of crisis? We've all felt threatened at times. We may feel intimidated by any unwelcomed change of circumstances. We may respond to divorce, career setback, or a sudden health challenge in such a way as to undermine our confidence and make ourselves afraid.

Let's take a closer look at that word, *intimidation.* Play with it. Remove the letters *id* from the middle of it and set them aside for a moment. Now, what word remains? *Intimation.* To intimate is to suggest or make known indirectly; to hint at something. A challenge or failure, or any crisis in life, is also an intimation to us, when we search for the opportunities hidden there.

Now retrieve the letters *id* and capitalize them: *I.D.* That, of course, is the abbreviation for *identification.* What is your identity in times of crisis? Are you threatened and fearful, or are you, instead, a bold seeker of the positive possibilities inherent in any ordeal?

Intimidation and intimation are two powerful words. Which one is used most often in your mental vocabulary? One will deny, the other affirm, your innate creative resources. *Choose your words carefully.*

Whenever doubt or fear call you, simply let your internal answering machine take it, and reply with this message: "Sorry, I'm fulfilling my potential right now. Take my number off your list—and don't ever call me again."

Choose Optimism for Mental Health

For each positive, a cynic can point to the negative. An optimist knows every negative contains a positive. Both are correct, but only one enjoys a healthy mind and a happy, productive life.

Anyone who dwells on life's unpleasant aspects is a starving person seated in a fine restaurant for a free meal, angry for being served bread that wasn't warm.

I once knew a knowledgeable man I'll call Don. His mind retained virtually everything he read, and the broad range of his education was impressive. But all that knowledge hadn't brought him much wisdom.

Don was a cynic.

For him, positive thoughts stopped in for a visit; negative thoughts took a permanent room upstairs. He found only fault with the world, so his inner world was pretty sorry too. He avoided the fear and discomfort associated with personal growth by withdrawing into himself and complaining about all that was wrong with the world. Certainly, he could cite plenty of examples!

But how does someone show such a lack of love for him or herself and others, ignoring the value and beauty of what many of us consider the finer things of life: flower gardens, scenic views, libraries, art museums, theaters, concert halls, and such? A callous spirit grows to suffocate appreciation and gratitude—keys to happiness. You cannot effectively act as both Nature's work of art and Her art critic. Either live and breathe Her creativity or tear yourself apart. Which course of action will you choose?

Don preferred the security of a known ditch to the adventure of an unknown road. "I can't change who I am," he argued. By saying that, Don reduced himself, intellectually, to the lowest level. "I can't change" makes about as much sense as "I can't blink." It really means "I *won't* change." The potential to change is built into us, like eyelids that open and close. We just need to make a decision and perhaps a more determined effort to accomplish the change. If we won't change, we've denied our potential.

Frankly, to be around Don for any length of time was both frustrating and emotionally draining. His attitude about himself, and life, was self-crippling. But he refused to seek help. Don saw himself as a failure, and he was one—by choice. "Cynic" is just another name for someone who has given up. However, if a seed of desire, no matter how small, still exists within, it can be nurtured and grown.

Healthy-thinking people patiently lay one brick of positive action upon another to create a larger, stronger self. Distance yourself from negative people who would pick away at your mortar rather than encourage you or help you lay more positive bricks.

Know that a certain percentage of people will always disagree with you, regardless of what action you take. Some of them may enviously laugh and jeer at you from the sidelines—precisely because they're on the sidelines! If others criticize your efforts, they always say more about themselves than they do about you. It's just a reflection of their unhappy thinking. If they were happy themselves, they would look for the good and applaud you.

Egotism Has No Place in Our Lives

A few years ago, I visited a large art show where the work of a fine watercolorist caught my attention. The detail in his paintings was exquisite and I felt moved to tell him so.

"It's wonderful to see the depth of realism you capture with your watercolors," I said. "Being a colored pencil artist myself,

I can appreciate the talent and time involved in creating such detailed work. Your paintings are beautiful."

He looked down his nose at me and said sarcastically, "Well, you have to learn to draw before you can paint." He then turned away.

I stood there feeling stung and dazed. "What's with this guy?" I wondered. "Here I've just paid him an honest, sincere compliment, and he responds by insulting me!" I left his booth thinking, "Wow! What an unhappy man he must be. How sad."

People at peace with themselves don't feel compelled to belittle anyone. A sturdy fabric of self-confidence is never woven from threads of inferiority put on others. That talented, but pompous, watercolorist who dismissed me with a verbal slap needs help and loving kindness, but he'd probably refuse it. Egotism often masks insecurity.

Puffing up your ego in an effort to feel better about yourself is somewhat like upgrading a wardrobe to improve the health of a deceased person just before the viewing. It's all show. There's no substance to it.

Talented people who find joy in their work seldom display egos. They quietly go about their business, content to be conduits for creativity. They're humbled by the realization that creativity flows through them from some mysterious, marvelous source.

Never allow yourself to be rattled by egotistical people who put down you or your efforts. Be above retaliation. Don't waste your valuable energy on them. Just wish them well and go on your way.

Eleanor Roosevelt kept this sign hanging in her Hyde Park, New York, home: "No one can make you feel inferior without your permission." Remember that whenever someone tries to diminish you. Take a comical view of such people. Arrogant egos stand all wobbly in the scheme of things, like a boastful drunk pulled to the side of the road and asked to walk a straight line.

Let Go of Regrets

We can stare at an old photograph all day and never change its composition, but we attempt to do just that if we've ever dwelled on the past with regret.

Through the years, I've met so many people tortured by regrets. They dissect the past as if it were their lab assignment. Even worse, they've barricaded themselves in the stale lab and refuse to come out to enjoy the fresh air of the present.

Two of the most powerful words in the English language are "let go." If you've made foolish choices and embarrassing mistakes in the past, congratulations! You've joined the ranks of everyone who has ever lived. However, if you have learned from your errors, made any needed adjustment, and left all your regrets behind, you are among the minority. Congratulations, again.

It's impossible to close the book on your past if you focus on, memorize, and repeat everything written there. Commit yourself now to letting go. If you need to make some apologies, do so. No one can travel back to yesterday, so why keep planning an itinerary for the trip?

Take Personal Responsibility

You can believe in your potential for growth, or you can tear yourself down with the words, "I can't." In life, we choose to be either architects or demolition experts. You are in control of which one you are. You can either wield the wrecking ball or build a meaningful life. It's up to you.

Not long ago, I watched a documentary program concerning the Revolutionary War and the birth of America. What impressed me most about our Founding Fathers was the great faith they held in our ability, as individuals, to govern ourselves.

When Thomas Jefferson wrote the Declaration of Independence, his expectations of the American people were high. He believed freedom required individuals to assume responsibility for their own lives, while dedicating themselves to the pursuit of excellence as a means of keeping the nation strong.

Were Jefferson to visit America today, he would be appalled by the growing number of people who no longer hold themselves accountable for their lives and behaviors. Ours has, unfortunately, become a society teeming with victims—many of whom are people who use their challenges as excuses for why they "can't" live the life they want. We've been challenged by dysfunctional parents, abusive spouses, alcoholism, drug abuse and other addictions, corporate downsizing, the tobacco industry, television violence, and even poverty. We talk about the disadvantaged as if their condition were a congenital trait, like blue eyes or freckles. We all have our challenges—big and small. Those who win use their challenges to strengthen themselves and, in overcoming them, springboard themselves to success.

The world doesn't owe anyone a living, and Father Time gives no one child support. Many whine and point fingers of blame at others for what are really their personal failures and an unwillingness to change themselves for the better. Choosing to play victim is just another way of saying, "The dog ate my homework." It is disempowering.

Refuse to hold yourself accountable for your failures and it's like standing in front of a mirror and denying your reflection. "But people do experience hard times and setbacks," critics would argue. "Shouldn't we offer them compassionate support?"

Of course! But what's the best way to do this? "Sink or swim" is the heartless advice given to those who struggle to stay afloat in troubled water. "If I can swim," we could say to them, "then you can swim too. Here's how you do it." No amount of commiseration or compassion alone will help anyone. The most compassionate message you can give to a person is: "I believe in you."

People will usually live up to—or down to—your expectations of them. "I believe in you" is no simplistic comment. It's a statement of faith and great compassion. To help people realize the vast power they possess to change themselves and their circumstances is an act of true kindness. To hold people accountable for their own behaviors is to give them respect and dignity. To expect the best from people is to show them love. You can teach people to swim, but you can't swim for them.

A Dangerous Super-Glue

The strongest glue in the world doesn't come in a tube or plastic bottle. The powerful ingredients consist of four simple words: "It's Not My Fault!" Using these words together is the surest way to keep yourself stuck wherever you are in life. They're guaranteed to immobilize you right on the spot.

Roberta was eight when she began playing the violin. Her passionate desire for playing was so strong that she practiced for hours on end. Her dedication brought forth a genuine talent.

At age 12, she was taking private lessons with a distinguished professor of music, whose guidance helped her enhance her knowledge and musical ability. By her senior year in high school, Roberta had won first chair in an All-State Orchestra, defeating many talented students for this coveted position.

She received scholarship offers from several colleges. During an audition for enrollment at one prestigious music school, the judges were suspicious that Roberta had broken the rules when she sight-read an unfamiliar composition perfectly. Her performance was so excellent, the judges thought that someone had sneaked the music to her prior to the audition! The stunning results of her second test, using different music, left the judges feeling apologetic—and astounded.

"That was my peak accomplishment," Roberta recalls today, at age 40. "Afterward, everything began to fall apart."

"My mother didn't want any of her kids to leave home," she shared. "Mom wouldn't accept that things change and life moves on. Looking back, I can now see how unhappy and manipulative she was. Her tears had a powerful effect on me. I felt guilty for wanting to go away to college."

"What about your father?" I asked her.

"Dad was working three jobs and couldn't be bothered. He found it easier just to agree with Mom."

Despite the scholarship offers, Roberta chose to enroll in a smaller music school within her state. She was miserable. "I resented my parents," she says, "actually blaming them for *my* decision not to attend one of the best-ranked music schools in the country—on a full scholarship!"

When Roberta told her parents she needed a better violin for scholastic competitions, they said the money wasn't available.

"Why didn't you take a part-time job and buy the violin yourself?" I asked her.

"It was easier to make excuses. Professionals need to play eight hours daily if they want to compete successfully. But I told myself it was my parents' fault that I wasn't practicing enough, because they wouldn't give me the proper instrument."

The university Roberta attended was known as a "party school," and unfortunately she joined the party with enthusiasm. Late night reveling and binge drinking soon hastened her academic decline.

"When professors criticized my performance, I accused them of being unreasonable and intolerant. What a great excuse-maker I was in those days," she says, shaking her head sadly. "I blamed my parents and uncaring professors—everyone but myself. Nothing was my fault."

Roberta quit college after her freshman year, moving into a modest apartment off-campus and taking a food server job to support herself. But her partying and drinking continued. "Alcohol gave me instant ease and comfort," she remembers. "It deadened the pain."

She also sought escape from herself in a string of relationships with men who had losing attitudes and behaviors. "I made terrible choices in men," she says. "Of course, I didn't see things that way at the time." She just blamed men.

For Roberta, her "It's Not My Fault!" super-glue kept her stuck in a world where she believed family, professors, and the men she dated all conspired to victimize her. "Everyone took advantage of me," she says, "and I felt oh so sorry for myself!" She had hit bottom.

Roberta sought treatment for alcoholism and began her long road to psychological recovery. "To face my life honestly wasn't easy," she admits. "Old ways of thinking are comfort-able—even when they're destroying you." But she stopped using the super-glue of blame.

Sober for 20 years, Roberta is now a happily married mother of two, whose home-based sales business is thriving. (She also plays violin in a community orchestra.) "I learned the hard way that my thoughts create everything in my life," she says. "*I'm* the one responsible for the kind of life I live."

Accountability is the only effective solvent for detaching yourself from the super-glue of blame. Bitterness, resentment, and envy also dissolve when the decision is made to accept full responsibility for the who, what, where, and why of your life.

"Responsibility educates," wrote 19th Century reformer Wendell Phillips. The decision to assume responsibility for all your failures, as well as your successes, is your most vital tool for rapid learning and personal growth. It greatly strengthens your capacity to live a rich, rewarding life.

Take Charge—*Get Out From Under the Circumstances*

"If only my situation were different, I could do what I want." Sound familiar? Perhaps you've said this to yourself. If your brain were a clock radio, this statement would be the snooze button.

Wake up!

Thinking, action-oriented people don't shrug their shoulders and accept their lot in life. They demand a lot from life and themselves—and they get it.

"If only my situation were different" is as though your pre-sent circumstances were flypaper, and you were the fly. Your life, as it exists today, is a partially completed notebook. You grip the pen and, if you're not happy with what you've been writing, turn the page to start a new chapter.

Remember when, as a kid in school, you committed some minor infraction and the teacher made you write something like, "I will not talk in class," one hundred times? Along with writer's cramp, you also experienced the joy of taking the paper home for your parents to sign.

Well, here we sit today with life's notebook, pen in hand, and what one sentence do many of us repeatedly write? "If only my situation were different, I could do what I want."

Page after page may be filled with this mantra of complete resignation. If we insist on scrawling the same thoughtless, negative sentence, at least let's be honest in our writing. The statement could read: "In my present situation I'll do nothing to achieve what I want."

Some people say they want to soar, but it can't be done without the wings of self-belief. Get out from under the circumstances and make something good happen in your life.

Responsibility is a boomerang. If you throw it hard at others, or at past or present circumstances, be prepared to duck. It will surely come back.

Take complete responsibility for your life. Know that you can never again honestly blame your failures or unhappiness on anyone, or anything, but yourself. Realize that all of the choices you've made have led you precisely to the place you now occupy. Your choices—not circumstances—have created what and where you are today. Those who claim to be the victims of circumstance assume the impossible—that they've lost their innate power to choose. That's just not true. You *can*—choose!

Playwright George Bernard Shaw said, "People are always blaming their circumstances for what they are in life. I don't believe in circumstances. The people who get on in this world are the people who get up and look for the circumstances they want and, if they can't find them, make them."

"But circumstances are often out of our control," one man said to me recently. "They can dictate our lives," he argued. "We don't always have choices."

Granted, some people are in more challenging situations than others. Some have higher hurdles to get over. But it's how we choose to deal with them that determines our ultimate success or failure. The fact of the matter is that the most successful people usually come from the ranks of the most challenged.

In the ballpark of any circumstance, the right attitude will always hit the ball—and maybe even a home run.

One of my favorite people is Abraham Lincoln. We hear his name today and he may not seem real to us. He's a legend, seemingly larger than life. But Lincoln was human. Throughout his life, he suffered periods of depression so severe he'd remain in bed for days at a time. As president, he was not well liked. Editorial cartoonists of his day often portrayed him as a baboon. Lincoln watched helplessly as first one son—and later another—died in childhood from disease. His wife, Mary, was a mentally unstable woman, known to embarrass and humiliate him in public. Lincoln presided over a nation being torn in two by the Civil War. He saw more than 600,000 of his fellow Americans die in that conflict.

But Lincoln understood that it's our responses to the challenges of life that either elevate or destroy us. "Most people," he said, "are about as happy as they choose to be."

Lincoln stands as a shining example of how to take responsibility in life. He chose to endure. Take responsibility for your life and the potential within you to overcome any obstacle to success. The only limits on you, ultimately, are those you place upon yourself by not believing in yourself. Remember, you *always* have choices.

To dwell on what you would do "if circumstances were different" is to sit out in the rain, surrounded by closed umbrellas, and just daydream about how much better you'd feel if you were dry.

"If circumstances were different" is a sensible lament only if you find yourself bound and gagged with a bomb in your lap— and that bomb has just stopped ticking.

"I have no choice" is just another choice.

Don't Stand Too Close

Imagine yourself in an art museum. Your face is positioned two inches away from a fine painting as you stare at what appears to be a glob of some color brushed hastily onto the canvas. "This Rembrandt doesn't do much for me," you may think to yourself. "I don't see what all the fuss is about."

Take a few steps back and, suddenly, that brushstroke begins to make some sense to you. Put a little more distance between you and the painting, and that glob of color melds perfectly with the others to create a beautiful work of art.

As observers of life, all of us are probably guilty, to some degree, of standing too close. We sometimes take life out of context. Caught up in our daily routines and responsibilities, preoccupied with our challenges, we may fail to step back and see ourselves for what we really are: part of the masterpiece of the world—a living, breathing work of art.

Your life and the planet on which you live hold little meaning when separated from their broader context. You need to stand back each day to see yourself as the marvelous brushstroke you are. Step back farther and understand that you also hold your own palette, brushes, and an infinite combination of colors for your use. In reality, you are both paint and painter, here to make your own work of art within this art gallery called the world.

Playwright Neil Simon says that his sense of humor is due, in part, to an ability to step back and observe himself during moments of personal challenge. This detachment, in the middle of emotional times, allows him to see virtually any situation from a comical perspective.

To change ingrained patterns of negative thought and action, we need to engage in this kind of objective observation. Unproductive attitudes and behaviors, many of which we've been hauling around with us for years, are best dealt with from a fresh and distant point of view.

When you practice becoming the mental eyewitness to your moments of fear and negativity, questioning the "why" of any insecure feelings you may have, you'll begin to see the role that unthinking habit has played in sabotaging your potential for growth. A more objective and amused recognition of your personal weaknesses gives you new insight into those old patterns of thought, enabling you to more easily break away from the hold they once had on you.

Only when we fully understand the what and why of self-limiting attitudes are we able to change in positive, lasting ways.

Look Outside Yourself

We all have so much untapped potential. Accept yourself. Any elements of weakness or inferiority you feel can be offset by learning to focus on your inner strengths. Yes, we all have them! Don't deny any insecure facets of your personality that you may have. Acknowledge them. They re part of you, but they are not all you are. To be limited by feelings of deficiency is to ignore the potential for greatness that's also part of you. Utilizing more of it can bring you greater inner peace and fulfillment.

Why is it so easy for many of us to view our flaws honestly, yet have such difficulty seeing the potential excellence inside? All of us need to take a realistic approach to what's positive about ourselves. There are elements in each of our personalities that we can build upon to achieve success. To excel, you need to focus on and develop your inner strengths and then give of yourself to others, directing your positive qualities into something larger than yourself. By looking outward, not inward, we soon forget any insecurities we may have and begin to know the joy of contributing our unique, desire-born talents as we help others.

As a young man, Abraham Lincoln was a self-absorbed neurotic. At age 32 he said, "I am now the most miserable man living. If what I feel were equally distributed to the whole human family, there would not be one cheerful face on earth."

It's hard to believe this is the same man who grew to become one of the greatest presidents the U.S. has ever known. You can more easily understand Lincoln's transformation from a self-absorbed introvert to skillful leader when you see the greater causes to which he eventually dedicated his life. By focusing outward, Lincoln brought forth the best from within himself, and you can too. Like he did, dedicate your life to a good cause.

Develop a Sense of Humor

One personality trait essential to our sanity is a healthy sense of humor. Lincoln certainly had that. His self-deprecating humor and a willingness to accept his own deficiencies were part of his greatness. A woman once accused him of being two-faced. "Madam," he said, "if I had two faces, do you think I would choose this one?"

Humor is our internal mechanic, free for us to cultivate. It inspects, adjusts, and lubricates our mental machinery to keep it in good working order.

When we maintain a spirit of playfulness, it keeps alive that child-like sense of awe and wonder about life and our own potential as human beings. Humor cultivates our imagination and nurtures our creative spontaneity. Coupled with passionate desire, these are invaluable tools in the pursuit of our dreams.

Humor relieves tension by removing us from ourselves and making us—like Neil Simon—detached observers. From this perspective, we can usually think more clearly about problems. The detachment humor provides gives us a pair of fresh eyes.

Humor reins in our ego and feelings of self-importance. It helps us maintain a healthy attitude about life and our place in the world. If you can't laugh at yourself, you're missing out on some of the funniest comedy material available. A sure sign of self-acceptance is the ability to laugh at yourself. To do that, you need to let go of your ego, step outside of yourself, and take an objective look at who you really are. That requires a degree of maturity we all need to cultivate.

Finally, humor touches emotions that are felt universally. Victor Borge liked to say, "The shortest distance between two people is a good laugh." Through humor we recognize our common fears and insecurities. Good comedy makes for ca-maraderie.

It is important to live larger than yourself, to dedicate your desires to serving others. Focus on others. It's essential to becoming truly successful. You'll also find it much more fun than just being self-absorbed. As you serve others, you'll get to observe the world from their unique perspectives. You'll learn about so many new things—it'll make your life much more interesting.

You may consider yourself to be a little shy. Many people are, even if they appear not to be. By nature, I'm a shy person. That shyness is a personality deficiency I recognize, and I'm working on it. Part of the process is writing this book. I refuse to allow my self-absorption, which causes my shyness, to detract from the potential good I can do.

Some time ago, I discovered this story by Margaret Lee Runbeck in a yellowed, 1947 edition of *Reader's Digest*. She recalled being a shy, awkward young woman of 18, sitting on the auditorium stage at her high school graduation. Because of her scholastic achievement, Margaret was assigned the task of delivering the valedictory address. She was a nervous wreck.

On stage with her that day was the commencement speaker, in whom she confided, "I'm scared to death." He smiled kindly, and this is what he said:

> "I'll tell you a secret, and then you'll never need to be scared again. Everyone on earth is shy, self-conscious, and unsure of himself. Everybody's timid about meeting strangers. So if you'll just spend the first minute you're in the presence of a stranger trying to help him feel comfortable, you'll never suffer from self-consciousness again."

Margaret Lee Runbeck always remembered that friendly stranger's advice. She applied it that day and throughout her life. Margaret often wished she could have recalled his name, to thank him for his kindness. Many years later, while cleaning out her attic, she came across her old, high school Commencement Day program. On the front cover it said, "Commencement Address, by Assistant Secretary of the Navy, the Honorable Franklin D. Roosevelt."

"The only obstacle that really stands in your way is you. Some catch the football of opportunity only to block and tackle themselves."

—Bruce Garrabrandt

Chapter 2

What's Your Purpose?

*"True happiness and joy is in the pursuit of
your dream—your purpose—when you choose
the path that's right for you."*
— Bruce Garrabrandt —

A sk people what they want and you'll often hear, "I want to be happy" or "I want to be rich." They may be forever frustrated, because directly seeking happiness and money does not lead to a happy, prosperous life. They are by-products of pursuing your purpose and can come only with achievement. Don't confuse them with goals. Take a direct aim at happiness, and you'll instantly lose sight of the target. But do what's right for you, and happiness and joy, as well as monetary rewards, can be yours along the way.

Dr. Benjamin Spock, the baby doctor, expressed it well. "Happiness is mostly a by-product of doing what makes us feel fulfilled." I also like Bette Davis's thoughts on the subject. "To fulfill a dream," she said, "to be allowed to sweat over lonely labor, to be given the chance to create, is the meat and potatoes of life. The money is the gravy."

Happiness and money can be found in the process of doing. The search for happiness in money or material possessions themselves can be, at best, fleeting. It is like a dying man's last wish for a new mattress.

It's foolish to look for personal fulfillment in things. "If I could just have that new car, house, relationship, or job, I'd be happy." Wrong. You may have monetary happiness. But when the novelty wears off, you'll be looking for happiness in something else—which can be a virtually endless cycle.

Look at people who achieve sudden fame. The money pours in, and they can buy anything they want. I could fill the rest of this book with names of men and women who "have it all" yet still feel miserable. Along with all the new possessions came their same, old, flawed ways of thinking. They were always looking outside themselves for happiness.

Such people are decorating a house with no foundation. They can paint it, landscape it, and fill it with the finest furniture—only to see it collapse. No amount of possessions can furnish the empty space within.

An English professor I knew in college, Dr. Philip Flynn, described this challenge as "the little voice." It tells us we could be happy if only we had that new ___. So we may be spending our lives chasing after things, expecting possessions to bring us fulfillment. But that restless, little voice always returns to tell us we need even *more* things. The race often ends only when we do.

Here's a short verse I wrote to describe the situation:

> *A change in looks*
> *Or what you own*
> *Or work you choose to do,*
> *A move from here to somewhere else*
> *And still you live with you.*
> *The only change that really counts*
> *When all is done or said,*
> *Is ever hid from public view*
> *And happens in your head.*

Those who believe they need a change of scenery need to look first to their inner landscapes. Searching for external answers to internal challenges is like playing the piano with a guitar pick. As the cartoon character Ziggy says, "Wherever I go, there I am!"

Nothing can bring happiness or joy to us. We are the vehicle in which it exists. Take any desire you may have to acquire more money, material possessions, leisure, or something else and direct that hunger toward the accumulation of more knowledge about yourself. Increase ownership of your inner strength and potential, grow your store of talents and abilities, gain increased wisdom, and develop more compassion for others, and you'll become one of the richest people in the world. While money does matter, your courage, character, consistency, compassion, and creativity always matter more.

Find Your Passionate Desire

What are *you* passionate about? The answer is different for everyone reading this book. Each of us is born with passions and desires, and we're here to develop them. In that process, our joy, happiness, and prosperity will come. They are our gifts—the results of which are our contributions to the world. Are you using your gifts or just playing with the packaging material?

Given the choice, what would you love to be doing? Stop and take some time to answer that. Then, when you believe in yourself and take responsibility for your life, you'll know that you've already been given the choice to do what you love.

"Success," according to Malcolm Forbes, "follows doing what you want to do. There is no other way to be successful." What you're passionate about is what you need to do. This desire will see you through any frustrations and setbacks you'll face while striving to reach your goal or dream. It's an ingredient essential to all success.

"I don't want people who want to dance," said choreographer George Ballanchine, "I want people who *have* to dance."

Frank Sinatra once listened to his son deliver a half-hearted singing performance and yelled at him, "You're contributing nothing if you aren't excited by what you're doing." Whatever you love to do, whatever subject excites you, whatever that gift is, pour yourself into it! Give it your all. Do what is in your heart of hearts to do.

The rewards for labor are to be found in the labor itself. Leisure gives you the momentary pleasure of a passing good time. Ongoing satisfaction and joy come with a loving commitment to your work. "The only true happiness," said English poet William Cowper, "comes from squandering ourselves for a purpose." Work done just for a paycheck is called making a living. Work done for the pleasure or joy of doing it is called creating a passionate life—*the journey is the success.*

Life without passionate desire is like a monochrome rainbow—dull and boring.

What Are Your Strengths?

As an artist, I see no reason to be egotistical about being able to draw well. I'm no better than anyone else. I just do what I've always believed I would enjoy doing. My desire drove me to do it and become well-practiced at it, that's all. So-called talented individuals with large egos have lost their perspective. They're just regular people like you and me, doing something very well that they, hopefully, love to do. They could be humbled by the truth that talent has a creative source much bigger than any ego's inflated feelings of self-importance.

Ego, self-focused, struts back and forth in the storefront window, while humility busily takes inventory, offers service to others, and provides the goods.

Our commonality as human beings could well keep ego under control. But recognizing our uniqueness and the contributions we have to make as individuals could inspire us to expand our imaginations. We are ordinary people in possession of extraordinary potential. Life, at its best, is the solitary discovery and unfolding of that potential, a dedication to personal development and making a difference. That's where true happiness, joy, and fulfillment are found.

Ditch the silly, romantic notion that "artists," in any arena, are born and not made. They need to be both—and you can count yourself among this group if you choose to do so, no matter what your vocation.

Everyone has an aptitude to do at least one thing well. But you can only play to your strengths when you have the desire to recognize them. Step outside yourself and examine, as objectively as possible, what you do well. We're often blind to our own natural abilities—we may overlook what comes easily to us. Even worse, we may tend to focus on our personal weaknesses, allowing any feelings of awkwardness and insecurity to define us. But why take the best in ourselves for granted?

While agreeing that each of us has a purpose for being alive, "I still don't know mine" is how many respond to hearing that. People smile when I tell them that everyone has the potential to do at least one thing well and with great joy. "I wish I knew what that one thing was," they say with a laugh. Wishing is for those who get results from genies and lamp-rubbing. The rest of us need to act.

Think seriously about yourself. Examine your personality— the nuts and bolts of who you are as a person—and compile a list of what you determine to be your positive traits. What do you like about yourself? Which subjects do you enjoy learning about? What pursuits have brought you the most satisfaction in life? ("I don't know" does not qualify as a legitimate response to any of the above questions.)

Be honest about it. Take time to identify your personal strengths, then commit yourself to utilizing and fine-tuning them. Nurture and develop these good qualities of yours in ways that will provide a rewarding career or business of joyful work. Not only is this within your power to do, it's also your responsibility.

"Why was I born?" is a common lament. Well, who, but the lamenter, is in a better position to discover the answer?

"The best is yet to come" is true only when you choose to explore the best within yourself and follow your heart.

Look at the ears of an elderly person. Notice how large they are? The cartilage which forms them continues to grow throughout life. (Too bad listening skills don't always expand along with the cartilage.) What's true for ears also holds true for personalities. The prominent traits we possess today will become more pronounced over time. Both sweet and sour dispositions expand with age.

What characteristics about yourself will others see accentuated in you? Kindness? Curiosity? Cheerfulness? If you haul around bitterness, impatience, or laziness, this mental baggage will really weigh you down in later years.

Assess your basic personality. Is it positive or negative? Your dominant attitude is surely a long-term investment—good or bad—in yourself.

Do We Find Ourselves or Make Ourselves?

Whenever someone tells me "I need to find myself," I endeavor to be helpful. "Have you checked between the couch cushions?" I ask. "Where was the last place you remember seeing yourself?"

Many people drift for years with the belief that their real lives will begin the moment they finally find themselves. Remember, the acorn does not search outside itself to become an oak tree!

Successful people don't find themselves; they *make* themselves by the strength of their desire. It's a process of learning and growth, a daily act of creation which requires concentration, patience, and dedication to purpose.

Are You Waiting for the Bus?

Imagine yourself sitting at a bus stop, miles from civilization. There you wait, but no bus comes. You stand up and begin to pace the dirt road. You're tired, hungry, and irritable. You look up the road and long for a bus to appear from over the hill, but still no bus comes. You shake your fist at the sky for being left stranded out on that road. Eventually you lose consciousness, never knowing that a bus was parked just over the hill—waiting for *you* to drive it.

What About Starving Artists?

Dreams are fragile things. Without focus and desire, and the encouragement and appreciation of others, they can easily shatter and be lost forever. We may justify that loss by telling ourselves "it wasn't meant to be." We might think we weren't being realistic with our aspirations, so we end up settling for something less. We may stay on practical, proven paths, even though we might be sad, frustrated, or mentally tortured by our sense of loss. After all, we may surmise, life is serious business. We've probably been taught that we need to get a good education, find a decent job, and earn enough money to live comfortably. These might have become our goals and, as a result, our dreams may have died.

If life were a high school metal shop, a few students would strive to build bridges, but the rest would settle only for making ashtrays. How sad.

We only have a certain number of years to live and we don't know how long that will be. So why not go for the dream and do it now? I'm not suggesting that we ignore the responsibilities of life. Dream responsibly! We can fulfill our obligations as self-reliant adults and *still* get to where we want to be.

Giving creativity free rein and allowing ourselves to believe in a dream isn't irresponsible behavior. It's just the opposite. As stated earlier, it's your duty to pursue a constructive passion—to nurture your gifts. No one else can do it for you.

I hear a lot about "starving artists." Do you know who the real starving artists are? They're the people who deny their dreams and fail to become the best they can be. They may be earning huge sums of money; their lives may be filled with material luxuries; they may eat in only the finest restaurants, but they're starving inside. If the artist within you, the creative dreamer, is not permitted to grow, then an important part of you is starving.

One of the most pleasing and happiest moments in my life came when I received the results of a personality test given to employees at the newspaper where I used to work. My answers to the battery of questions on this test placed me under the classification, "Uncontrollable Dreamer." How had I been able to hold down a job in newspaper advertising for thirteen years, given the fact that I was an uncontrollable dreamer?

A newspaper advertising representative spends a good part of each day on the road, seeing clients and helping them to develop advertising campaigns. Not chained to an office desk, I learned to work efficiently, fulfilling the responsibilities of my job early enough to still have an hour or two of free time on most days.

Through a dozen years in libraries and coffee shops, I used that time to read countless books, write several volumes of fiction and nonfiction, and turn my artistic abilities into a profitable career with a series of wildlife prints. Weekends were spent at juried arts and crafts festivals, evenings and early morning hours were devoted to cutting picture mats, making frames, and cutting glass.

"What you do instead of your work is your real work," says film critic, Roger Ebert.

I never shortchanged my employer, and I suggest you don't either. Strong activity management skills enabled me to develop many new accounts and set sales records, yet still have time to pursue my dreams. I didn't think much about this at the time, but the "uncontrollable dreamer" in me had naturally gravitated toward a job providing some degree of creative freedom.

Perhaps you're thinking, "Sure...it's easy to pursue your dream when you have that much free time during the day." While most people may not be in such a situation, ways can *always* be found to dedicate one or more hours to your goals daily. I'll describe some of these for you later.

Set Goals that Support Your Desire

The goals we set for ourselves need to support our desires. Goals need to be formulated with an understanding of our innate strengths. We all possess natural proclivities which, when nurtured and developed, can translate into a high level of proficiency and enjoyment.

If your heartfelt desire is acorns, don't strive to create a forest of pines.

"I want to win the Pulitzer Prize" is a huge goal, but taken one step at a time, could be realized. "I want to build a successful career or business, and earn a tremendous income doing it," is a great goal. "I will win an Oscar" is a great desire that can lead to becoming an accomplished actor. "I want to cure cancer" is an incredible goal, yet somebody's going to do it.

While having enthusiasm and taking action are essential for success, they're not enough. You need to direct these two forces into working smart. This can mean networking and associating with other like-minded people. As the saying goes, "Always roll your snowballs *down*hill."

Whatever dream you choose to pursue, though, needs to provide you with an ongoing sense of accomplishment, not just a few moments of applause. When your fulfillment comes with the doing, you'll be living your dreams.

Vocation and Vision

"We can't all enjoy prestigious careers or businesses" people have told me. "Some of us are destined to collect garbage, dig ditches, and work the assembly lines—jobs which don't exactly make your life as you would like."

We often link career or business happiness to professions which seem glamorous. People hunger for glamour because it looks attractive and exciting and easily captures their attention. But glamour is always a fluff food. Take a bite and feel it dissolve, like cotton candy, on your tongue. It can't sustain you. You need something more substantial from life's menu— something more meaningful.

Some people think a prestigious career or business is the answer to their dreams. But prestige is not synonymous with fulfillment. Would you rather be a renowned but jaded professional, who sees work as "drudgery for big dollars," or an upbeat sanitation worker who finds gratification in doing his job well? Your vision makes all the difference in the world.

What you do always holds less significance than how you do it. A change in attitude can transform you more dramatically than can any new career or business.

People with vision see their work as an opportunity to serve. They interact with coworkers and their community on a personal level, knowing that a loving outlook provides deep meaning to what they do.

"We cannot do great things in life," said Mother Teresa. "We can only do small things with great love."

Even the humblest of tasks—such as sweeping a sidewalk—can be performed with love.

Opportunity waits at our feet as we squint to look for it on the horizon. This is especially important to remember if you're working toward a career or business change. Such an undertaking may require years of effort before you achieve your dream. Meanwhile, your present job or business can be viewed in a broadened, more creative context. Wherever you are today, it's likely that greater reward may be found in providing more and better service to others.

Any job or business, or any activity, done with love, makes a positive difference. Be kind and compassionate in all that you do. Strive to make this attitude the whole of your being, incorporating it into all that you do. This is your calling, no matter what your job or business. "Every calling is great when greatly pursued," wrote Oliver Wendell Holmes, Jr.

Now let me tell you about Sid, once a tollbooth attendant on New Jersey's Garden State Parkway. Does anyone think of such a job as glamorous? Of course not. Every day you sit in a cramped, noisy little booth, breathing exhaust fumes from the cars and trucks, taking money and giving change endlessly, all day long. Boring, right? Well, not for Sid. His goal was to see that every driver who passed through his tollbooth left with a smile. Always upbeat, never complaining, he was genuinely interested in people, laughing and joking with them, taking time to learn a little something about their lives.

Sid seemed to know everybody. Having a problem with your car? Sid would recommend an honest mechanic. He liked to help people. If he discovered you worked locally, he might surprise you some morning by delivering a box of donuts to your office. Because he made a habit of handing out candy to kids, Sid enjoyed a wide reputation as "that great guy on the Parkway who gives stuff away."

Sid's coworkers loved him too. He always volunteered to take the busiest tollbooth lanes. He managed to find happiness in and give great joy to a job which most people would consider mundane. Significance can be found in any activity when it is performed with a loving spirit.

What Can You Contribute?

"What do we live for," asked writer George Eliot, "if not to make the world less difficult for each other?"

And Oscar Hammerstein II observed, "There is a very real relationship, both quantitatively and qualitatively, between what you contribute and what you get out of this world."

Think of your life purpose as one of creating a meaningful legacy. What can you contribute to those who'll follow you? What talent, i.e., desire, lies within you that you can tap into? We can be creative contributors whose work, in one form or another, will survive us. That needs to be our mission here. That's what ennobles us as human beings, gives purpose to our lives, and brings lasting happiness and joy.

People long for happiness in this life. George Bernard Shaw noted, "We have no more right to consume happiness without producing it, than to consume wealth without producing it." Be a productive contributor. It's the rent we're meant to pay for the space we occupy here. Is your rent overdue? Are you current in your contributions?

What do we own? We can only claim ownership to the deeds we perform. "Actions speak louder than words" the saying goes.

"Well done is better than well said," wrote Benjamin Franklin. Our individual potential, acted upon in a spirit of faith and goodness, is all we really own. Actions are our possessions. Through them we expand beyond skin and bones to touch the lives of others and make a difference in the world.

Think of historical figures whose lives we admire and respect. The most influential have always been those men and women whose desire-born talents and abilities were used in service to others, weren't they? Each of us has the power to make meaningful contributions to life.

Seeds of great potential have been sprinkled into our hearts. It's tragic when we don't realize this, because we won't germinate. With the flowering of what is best within us comes the deepest satisfaction and peace life can provide. Squander the opportunity and you lose sight of your purpose for being here, and the happiness and joy that can be yours goes away.

Some time ago, I came upon this quote from composer Gian-Carlo Menotti who said, in one sentence, what I've been trying to convey: "Hell begins on the day when God grants us a clear vision of all that we might have achieved, of all the gifts which we have wasted, of all that we might have done which we did not do."

What Will Your Epitaph Be?

Congratulations! At no cost to you or your loved ones, a bronze plaque honoring your memory will one day be placed in a lovely public setting for millions of people to see. Chiseled into it will be your name and a single-line epitaph, succinctly describing how you lived your life. What will it say?

Which one of these epitaphs would you like to have to summarize your brief time here?

- She never really lived fully.
- He settled for mediocrity because it was easy.

- She never thought of anyone but herself.
- He looked forward to the future, when he would have time to enjoy life.
- She had a big dream but never bothered to take action to make it come true.
- He was in a rut.
- She escaped commitment to anyone or anything.
- He avoided introspective thought.
- She was in a great business but never really did what it took to build it.
- His relationships were superficial.
- She took more than she gave.
- He could have done so much more.

Or could you choose one of the epitaphs below as your own?

- He always did his best.
- Her greatest satisfaction came from helping others.
- He lived in each moment and found great joy there.
- She earned great money because she gave a lot to society.
- Money came while she worked at what she loved.
- He dealt with people fairly and honestly.
- She loved deeply and knew the rewards of commitment.
- He knew what he wanted to accomplish and changed the world as he did.
- His relationships were deep and abiding.
- She gave more than she took.
- He was in a great business where he helped people all over the world and lived his dream.

Like it or not, your life will write its own epitaph. Would you be gratified or embarrassed to have the whole world know it?

"**I**f you have half a mind to do something, your other half will see to it that nothing gets done."

—Bruce Garrabrandt

Chapter 3

Take Action and Grow

"It's never too late to act; it's always too late not to."
— Bruce Garrabrandt —

A good way to begin a chapter titled Take Action and Grow is to return to the challenge of *inaction*. Why might change be so challenging for us? Rather than living our dreams, we may be keeping them locked up inside us and doing nothing to achieve them. Excuses may be rushing to our defense, providing cover for an unwillingness to act.

Earlier we looked at how self-limiting attitudes can hold us back from success. Let's examine further some of the secret fears that may be responsible for what might be our chronic procrastination.

"My life will fall short of my dreams. I'm afraid of failure. I couldn't bear the disappointment."

"What if I *do* succeed? Then I'll always be expected to succeed."

"If I fail, people will see me as a failure. That would be humiliating."

Psychologists tell us that such fears often have their origins in childhood. Not even the best parents can get *everything* right. Our formative years, to some degree, were probably *mal*formative as well. Childhood insecurities, unfulfilled needs, and parental expectations may have caused us to adapt in inappropriate, self-defeating ways. Rational thinking is not the hallmark of a young child's mind, so our responses were emotional—survival techniques which may have served us well at the time.

Unfortunately, we can remain children in the ways we cope with fear. Well-established emotional outlooks and negative thought patterns are seldom analyzed. As adults, we might simply continue to do what worked for us as children. Instead of pursuing personal development, we may be clinging to *arrested* development. There might even be a snugness to our suffering.

The causes for procrastination are many and often complex. "Our reasons for procrastinating are as varied as people are different," says licensed psychologist Robert B. Simmonds. He publishes an informative newsletter titled *Emotional Wellness Matters.* In Vol. 5, No. 6, he says, "...it may help to see procrastination as a symptom of underlying personality issues," he says. "For example, negative self-esteem often plays a role in our tendency to put off accomplishing tasks. Sometimes we postpone our duties because we lack self-confidence or we feel that we might be rejected by others if we don't turn in a perfect job. Sometimes procrastination is a symptom of depression."

The following stories may remind you of people in your own circle of acquaintances or even yourself. Their names, circumstances, and many other significant details have been altered to protect their privacy. Their stories are presented to encourage your thinking about the ways in which your early life experiences may be negatively affecting your current adult behavior.

Jack was the oldest of seven children. His father, a notable professional, demanded much from him. As the first-born, Jack was expected to set a high standard of scholastic and athletic excellence for his siblings to follow. He grew up hearing little praise from his dad. All efforts to please brought some variation of "You can always do better." Pressure to excel took its toll on the boy's mental health.

Jack left home for college. Sensitive and brooding, he seemed adrift at school. Concentration on his studies was a real struggle. He turned to alcohol and spent most of his time watching television in the student lounge. Placed on academic probation, he did nothing to change his behavior and eventually dropped out.

Telling Jack to contemplate his tremendous potential would have sent him into a panic. With greater achievement, Jack feared that pressures to perform at a higher level would grow. Life would be too demanding. "Who needs that kind of stress?" he said. Jack's fear of success effectively immobilized him. Failure, for him, provided a form of relief.

Diane was intelligent, attractive, and terribly insecure. She felt uncomfortable making any decision alone. Her dependence on others' advice and opinions began early.

Diane's father was a chronic philanderer, often absent from home. Her mother, unwilling to divorce and break up the family, directed all love and attention toward Diane, the only child. She was domineering, involved in every aspect of her daughter's life. Not even Diane's clothing and hairstyle decisions were made without parental consultation.

Diane's compliance and passivity won her mother's praise and approval, but they transformed her into a young woman distrustful of her own opinions. Feelings of inadequacy even poisoned her potential romantic relationships with men. Whenever a man showed interest, Diane distanced herself, acting out a version of the famous Groucho Marx line, "I'd never join a club that would have *me* as a member." For Diane, the feeling was, "Why should I respect anyone who finds *me* lovable?"

People who feel unworthy or inadequate, like Diane, react to the claim, "You have great potential," with disbelief. To them, it's farfetched. They simply don't believe it. Within them dwells the constant fear, "I don't have what it takes. I'm not good enough."

Ted worked far below his creative and intellectual potential, in a routine job he performed exceptionally well. He often complained that his work didn't challenge him but, when opportunities for advancement came Ted's way, he always passed them up. Why did he choose to stay stuck?

Ted's childhood was lonely. An emotionally disturbed younger brother received most of his parents' attention, leaving Ted feeling unimportant. "They seemed to take for granted that I could handle myself without much help," he said. So he withdrew emotionally, creating a macho image of total self-assurance.

As an adult, Ted continued to wear this mask. He wasn't a risk-taker. Though bright and witty, he hunkered down in an efficient mediocrity. This may have been unfulfilling, but at least Ted felt in control. He hated his work, but he did it meticulously.

For Ted, personal development was too great a gamble. To step outside of what he did perfectly would expose his vulnerability. He might be criticized or attacked for his actions. He chose to stay positioned behind his armor of capability, despite the accompanying boredom and unhappiness. Personal growth for Ted meant the surrender of his long-standing fortress.

If you feel stuck, then your present circumstances are providing some kind of payoff or you wouldn't continue doing what you're doing. Security at all costs? Fear avoidance? The approval of others?

Imagine the worst that could happen if you actually *moved toward* your dream. "Do the thing you fear" isn't just good advice for the conquering of mild phobias. It's also an excellent way—in fact, the *only* way—to make positive changes in your life.

Do you harbor a long-time fear? If so, do you realize it can slam the door on your personal development, closing you off from a world of promise and possibility? Return to the observer approach described in *Chapter One*. "Catch yourself in the act" when you experience emotional, child-responses to fear. Exploring these feelings will position you to make affirmative changes in attitude and behavior. You grow by first understanding any immature accommodations to fear you may have developed, then by choosing to establish new, mature approaches to living.

This can be a challenging task but the payoffs to such positive change—personal freedom and fulfillment—are your rewards for committed effort. If, for some reason, you experience some backsliding, just pick up where you left off and go at it again.

In pursuing any worthwhile goal, "We need to separate our emotions from the task itself," writes Dr. Simmonds. "In fact, working at the task gives us a good opportunity to see what our emotions are and to confront them honestly. This then allows us to learn where the feelings are coming from so that we can resolve them. Avoiding painful feelings lets them linger on into the future, but confronting them, especially with the help of a supportive and insightful therapist, can lead to emotional liberation." (*Emotional Wellness Matters, Vol. V, Number 6*)

We may look at certain people and say, "Wow! He (or she) has it all together." But life is paradoxical. In truth, those who basically have it together understand and accept that parts of themselves will *always* be at loose ends. That's the universal human condition. Everyone is a mixed bag of strengths and weaknesses. Virtually all of us feel vulnerable in some areas. No one is above it all.

When you see personal development as a natural, lifetime process which you are equipped to handle, you will have learned how to cultivate your desire. That, to borrow a movie title, is "as good as it gets."

How Do You Value Time?

You've heard the expression, "time marches on," and it certainly does that and more. Time dashes by—so use it wisely. Sometimes it may seem that the inner neck of life's hourglass has been sprayed with some sort of lubricant. Those grains of sand fall through so quickly. Life only gives us a guest room for the weekend, yet some of us live as if we owned the house. Well, obviously, we're not permanent residents here. The good news is that, while we're made of clay, we can sculpt ourselves into works of art.

"Everything comes to him who hustles while he waits," said Thomas Edison. Time is our most precious commodity, yet many of us don't utilize it well. Time is opportunity and squandered opportunity is a club, unfortunately, whose membership is too large.

Rudyard Kipling once said, "Fill the unforgiving minute with 60 seconds worth of distance run."

My dad was an English teacher. He liked to give his seventh-grade students a thought for the day. One of his favorites was the old Russian proverb, "A falling leaf is a whisper to the living."

Look around. Nature's design is one of planned obsolescence, but how many of us plan our lives with that in mind?

What if, all of a sudden, Father Time tapped you on the shoulder and said, "Your time is about up. You have only a year to live." What is it you long to do before you die? What dreams would you like to fulfill? What goals would you like to accomplish? What have you been meaning to do?

In the long-run, we learn that life is really a 50-yard dash. When the dust settles, we're all dust. What will have been your contribution to life? What will be your legacy left to grow? What would you like it to be?

Shakespeare was right—"Our time upon the stage is but an hour." In those precious moments we can:

- Strut and fret.
- Complain about the lighting.
- Paralyze ourselves with stage fright.
- Worry that we'll bump into the furniture.
- Obsess over our make-up.
- Continue to rehearse behind the curtain.
- Refuse to go on until we get a bigger dressing room.

- Stand in the wings and envy other actors.
- Allow ourselves to be strung and used as marionettes, or
- Do something else nonproductive.

We can also choose to walk directly into the spotlight and deliver a solid, memorable performance. What will you do on the stage of life?

Time Is Treasure

Consider the short span of your life in the immensity of time and you may feel you are insignificant. But the here-and-now is the only time that truly exists, existed, or will exist, and within this moment, your contribution can be significant.

The continual sweep of the second-hand turns all our moments to dust. What remains of anyone, ultimately, are the positive or negative effects of his or her actions.

"One day, I'll find the time." Have you ever said that? Well, you needn't search for it. The time is here and now. It's staring you in the face. What will you do with it? In the game of life, it's always your move.

I've always been keenly aware of the passage of time—too much so, actually. I'll tell you a secret. When I was in college, I used to go to the library and leaf through books of early photography. I was drawn to 100-year-old photographs of crowd scenes, Victorian men and women strolling along the boardwalk, marching in parades, or gathering under tents for revival meetings. I studied pictures of people who were full of dreams and desires, people that were no different than you and I, except they were gone. All of them. Dust.

I wondered what they did with their lives after the camera captured their images on film. What did they give to life? Who had they helped along the way?

I saw another old photograph recently when I stopped at a bagel shop for breakfast. While waiting at the counter, I noticed a large poster on the back wall. It pictured the interior of a train station. Printed beneath the photograph, in capital letters, was the caption, "GRAND CENTRAL STATION, 1934." The shot had been taken from above, looking at the rush of people below, as they made their way through the station. Shafts of afternoon sunlight from high windows shone down on the tiny figures, bathing them in a soft glow.

The scene had a special look. Caught on film in that long ago instant was an ephemeral quality, a feeling of sweet sadness. These people with all their plans, carried along by the hurried pace of daily living, didn't seem to notice what the photographer may have well understood: the almost mysterious beauty and fragile, fleeting nature of that particular moment—and of all the moments of our lives.

Studying photographs of people gone long before I was born, I became aware of the continuity of life. We all have a part to play. Today, and all the days of our lives, it's always our turn.

What difference can you make here? Answer that question, and then take your first step to act on it. Someday, someone may look at an old photograph of you and think, "What did this person do with his or her life?"

In Thornton Wilder's play, *Our Town*, a young woman, Emily, dies and is given the opportunity to return and observe any single day of her short life. When Emily wants to relive an especially happy day, she's told, "Choose an unimportant day. Choose the least important day in your life. It will be important enough."

Emily returns to a day from childhood and finds that she "can't look at everything hard enough." She's overwhelmed by the beauty of it all. "I can't go on," she says. "It goes so fast. We don't have time to look at one another." Emily discovers profound meaning in the smallest of moments, and she begins to cry. "I didn't realize...all that was going on and...never noticed."

Late in his life, Thornton Wilder wrote that *Our Town* was his "attempt to find a value above all price for the smallest events in our daily life." Imagine how much richer your life would be if you could hold in your mind the inestimable worth of each of your moments here. Time viewed as treasure would not be so casually spent.

Director Frank Capra's 1946 film, *It's a Wonderful Life*, is one of my favorites. It's a great story. A near suicidal George Bailey, played by Jimmy Stewart, is given a chance to see what life in his hometown would've been like had he never been born. George learns all the positive ways in which his actions influenced the people he knew. Without his caring presence on the scene, the lives of relatives, friends, and acquaintances were altered dramatically, and not for the better.

This thought-provoking movie can be a revelation to everyone. Each of us touches the lives of more people in more ways than he or she realizes. Even the smallest acts of kindness have a ripple effect which can reach countless others. So simple a gesture as a loving smile at the right moment may alter the life course of a stranger.

This isn't wishful thinking. It's a glimpse at the awesome power each of us holds, from moment to moment, to do either good or ill in this life. And like Thornton Wilder's character Emily, George Bailey comes to understand and value the profound meaning of all the moments of daily living. *It's a Wonderful Life* reveals the truth that life lived well is a wondrous process of learning to see, in glorious detail, what is in our immediate view. Each decent action or righteous choice you make is a test-flight of your soul's wings.

Have Your Ever Thought About the Underside of a Leaf?

When I give a motivational talk, I ask the people in the audience to complete an evaluation form at the conclusion of the presentation. Their comments and suggestions guide me to provide more helpful information in future programs.

During my talks, I refer to the brevity of life. This usually prompts at least one person to write the following on his or her evaluation sheet: "Inspirational message, but too much talk about death."

In truth, only a few minutes of my program deal with the subject of mortality. But some think that's a few minutes too many! Now, I'm not a morbid guy. My eventual demise is not a thought I like to dwell on. But acceptance of our mortality can be a great gift to ourselves. It can awaken us and prod us to set meaningful priorities. A healthy appreciation that our life will end can inspire us to realize more of life's possibilities.

Many years ago, the wife of a former Senator was stricken with terminal cancer. She wrote eloquently about living with the disease. One poignant comment in particular stays with me: "Only after being diagnosed with cancer did I discover the beauty of the underside of a leaf." With the threat of impending death, she awoke to the miracle of life and really began to see.

Your heightened awareness to life's majesty and mystery needn't wait for your closing days. Facing the reality of your ultimate death today can enhance the meaning of all your tomorrows.

Now Is the Time to Act—*What Are You Waiting For?*

I had the good fortune, as a kid, to have my great-grandmother live with us. I grew up under the same roof with a woman born in the 1870s. She was still alive and well in the 1970s. Her life spanned eras from the horse and buggy to lunar landings. It was a good, long life, yet even she was amazed by how quickly the years slipped away.

Living with someone that old was a blessing, because it shrank history for me. I realized, at an early age, that, even when you're here for a relatively long time in terms of human existence, you're not really here a long time. Life comes one day at a time, but the days seem to bunch together as we grow older. So get busy! Just because we come from dust and will someday return to dust, does not mean we need to be gathering dust while we're here.

How often do you catch yourself or someone else saying, "Someday, I'll...." Well, forget it! "Someday" becomes "never" before you know what's happened to you. I like to think of someday as a lifetime calendar with all the months and days missing.

No one stands the test of time by remaining seated. You can't make a deep impression on others while making a deep impression on your couch. "This is a world of action," said Charles Dickens, "and not for moping and droning in." We're creatures limited only by time and how we use it. Forget about what you're going to do someday. What are you doing now?

Good intentions alone can't accomplish anything. They are pleasant thoughts left to fade and be forgotten. Not acted upon, they let time flit away. It is useless to talk about a desired outcome if you're not moving toward it. It's just so much hot air.

Remember, there's always room at the top, but you can't get there sitting on your bottom. If you think you can do a thing, you can do it—unless all you do is *think* about doing it, in which case you can't. *Positive thinking without positive action is only wishful thinking.* Wishful thinking is all dressed up with no place to go.

All things begin in the brain, but don't let them end there. Wishes wobble. Actions advance!

In elementary school, we learned that a noun is a person, place, or thing. A noun is a person? How boring it is to be placed in the same category as a slab of concrete or a clump of sod! Let's think of ourselves as *verbs*—always in motion and taking creative action.

Life is movement. People are comprised mostly of water. When a body of water stops moving, what happens? It grows stale and polluted, and starts to smell bad. It breeds mosquitoes. Get moving. Live your life as a verb, an italicized, underlined verb—and put an exclamation point after it!

Get Off Your Assets—*Success Doesn't Offer Home Delivery*

Have you ever known people who thought their talents were obvious? They believed that opportunities would seek them out. One day, success would surely fall into their laps. But the only things to fall into their laps were pretzel crumbs when they parked themselves in front of the television every night.

Don't expect to be picked up and carried on the shoulders of success if you're sitting comfortably with the TV remote in your hand. Get off your assets!

During the Golden Age of Hollywood, stories circulated about pretty young women being discovered by talent scouts while bagging groceries in small town markets. The movie industry whisked them away and made them stars. Well, those days are pretty much over. And even if that isn't true, you need to act as if it were. The world is much too busy to take notice of how wonderful you are as you just sit there.

It seems obvious that getting where you want to go in life starts by moving from where you currently are. We all know people, though, who want to reach their desired destination without bothering to make the trip. We hear them dream, plan, and idly talk about where they long to be, as though this wishful thinking could somehow uproot the goal or dream and powerfully haul it to their present location.

Success doesn't offer home delivery. Would those who think success comes automatically ever expect food for next week's meals to make its own way into their refrigerators?

"Lights! Camera! Inaction!" A director would never yell this command on a movie set. The cost of poor or nonuse of actor and crew time is exorbitant. Procrastination would eventually close down production.

No one will use a bullhorn to tell you this, but the lights of possibility in your life are on and your days are rolling. You can't afford to mill around on the set; the cost is too high. You're allotted only a limited time for production. Use it wisely.

Take action!

Continue Your Education and Grow

Many of us tend to pack away our learning skills along with our diplomas. Become a lifetime student of personal development and all of life will be a supportive teacher. You don't have to spend a lifetime with yourself just as you are. Education and motivation enable you to choose better company.

In the same way that you can't bake a cake without the right ingredients, neither can you achieve a goal without the right knowledge. Immerse yourself in your subject of interest and study every aspect of it. You're doing more than simply acquiring information. All of those facts and insights bake inside your brain and form new ideas to help you develop your desire so you can reach your goals and dreams.

Build a foundation of research and new understanding. You can benefit from the knowledge of experts and those who've achieved the goal or dream you desire. Observe, listen to, and talk to successful people who are doing what you're interested in.

Learn from the great minds who came before you. Read! Their experience is yours for the taking. That's their gift to you. Don't let it grow dusty in a library or on your own bookshelf. Utilize it. "If a man empties his purse into his head," said Ben Franklin, "no one can take it away from him. An investment in knowledge always pays the best interest." Taking in new ideas and concepts stimulates your mind to think more creatively. Interact with what you read. Don't simply accept it as truth. Analyze what you learn and decide for yourself how to make it work for you.

The creation of a wholly original idea is impossible. Genius doesn't explode upon the scene from nowhere. What is viewed as original thought always arises from the reworking of earlier thoughts in new and improved ways. Brilliance, cleverness, and innovation aren't usually brought about by "bolt-from-the-blue" inspiration—although it can start this way, it usually doesn't. Chances are, if you postpone action until you feel inspired, you've taken a permanent seat in life's waiting room.

In what subject would you like to experience a stroke of genius? Study it deeply, until you become a walking encyclopedia. You'll discover the truth concerning genius. Neither glamorous nor original, it takes place when we accumulate borrowed thoughts, then blow the dust off them by refashioning these old ideas in innovative ways.

"I am more of a sponge than an inventor," said Thomas Edison. "I absorb ideas from every source. My principal business is giving commercial value to the brilliant but misdirected ideas of others."

Creativity is driven by your desire and comes with the imaginative use of that which already exists. Acquired knowledge, written in our own unique handwriting, i.e., from our own individual perspective, creates "original" thought.

I usually describe myself as a self-taught artist, but this is somewhat misleading. No one is ever really self-taught. I've learned from every artist whose work I admire because I had the desire to do so. Instructional art books, art galleries, and museums have provided me with tools as necessary as the paper and pencils I used to practice and sharpen my artistic skills.

Your originality will emerge with the intelligent use of your time and effort. While the adage "There's nothing new under the sun" is true, your imagination can alter the lighting in new and beautiful ways.

You *Can* Extend Your Life

Most of us want to live longer, right? We exercise, do our best to eat the right foods, and take vitamin and mineral supplements. This can certainly improve the quality of our lives—and maybe even add a few years. But can we expect to double or triple our lifespans? Perhaps not, although this may change as new longevity studies are conducted. But it is possible to extend life in another way.

While you may not be able to add years to your life, you can add more life to your years—by looking back and learning from those who came before you. In a very real sense, books can be your personal time machine, transporting you to other eras and places where you can meet people who cared enough to put thoughts and ideas into permanent form for your benefit. What a wonderful legacy they have given you. Virtually all the genius this world has ever produced is available for you to tap into, learn from, and use for your benefit.

Keep learning the ideas of great minds. Your own mind will continue to expand as you add centuries of breadth and depth to your life. Avail yourself of all the great teachers and leaders this world provides—both past and present.

I am thankful for those precious, desire-driven people whose words have touched my life and helped to point the way for me to achieve greater understanding. Dip into this vast reservoir of knowledge and drink from it daily. You'll be amazed by the number of different ways in which your life is inspired and changed for the better.

Turn off the television and read. Abraham Lincoln is whispering, "Spend an evening with me." Anne Morrow Lindbergh is tapping you on the shoulder, "I have something to tell you." Dale Carnegie is saying, "Listen to me and you'll have greater success." Og Mandino is asking, "Have you read my parables?" The list of individuals whose words can enrich your life is endless and growing all the time. Begin to extend your life. Consider the words of esteemed speaker and best-selling author Charlie "Tremendous" Jones, "The only difference between where you are now and where you'll be in the next five years will be the people you meet and the books you read."

A Roadblock to Action

If you think you might look silly doing something new, just say to yourself, "Who cares?" With that kind of attitude, you free yourself up to master almost anything. Sadly, some people's egos transform them into large, concrete barriers, blocking their road to personal growth. Could this be true for you? Most of us are reluctant to appear clumsy or awkward in any new venture. Self-consciousness may prevent us from accepting the fact that beginners generally look that way. It's the nature of starting anything new.

"A thing worth doing," wrote G.K. Chesterton, "is worth doing badly." It's fine to set a high standard for yourself, but it's quite unrealistic to expect the instant attainment of that standard. Patient acceptance of steady growth, which may seem slow at times, is needed. Along with that, the ability to use failure and frustration as fuel to feed your desire is essential for you to keep moving forward.

The idea of unlocking your creative potential can be intimidating if you compare yourself to experts whose work or accomplishments you admire. That's not comparing apples to apples. It's comparing apple seeds to apples! We forget that great artists, writers, business people, musicians—experts in every field—began by first doing it badly and persisting until they became proficient at it.

As a child with an insatiable curiosity, you demonstrated a comfortable awkwardness while learning from the world around you. You did it once and you can do it again.

Be Courageous

It can be challenging to alter your course and embark on a path to realize more of your potential—like entering an unfamiliar room in total darkness. You would expect to stumble into some furniture, so courage is essential. In the face of risk you also need to have faith. Relax, move forward, and accept that your shins may get bruised.

Keep a playful attitude as you feel your way around a new situation. You'll become familiar with the surroundings at your own pace, and with this knowledge your confidence will grow. Remember, no courage is needed where there is no fear. Taking positive action is always the best cure for overcoming fear.

"Dis" is an innocent sounding little prefix. It sits on page 642 of *Webster's Third New International Dictionary*. In Latin, it meant "apart, to pieces." Today we tack it onto the front of words to signify (1) reverse, (2) deprive of, (3) expel from, or (4) absence of.

Remember "dis" if you ever allow yourself to become discouraged.

Turning to page 745 of the same dictionary, I found a much healthier prefix, "en." What a powerful combination of two letters! It can mean (1) put on, (2) cause to be, (3) provide with, or (4) cover or surround thoroughly.

Let that *en*courage you!

Knowledge and Opportunity Call for Action

"Knowing is not enough," said German poet Goethe, "we must apply. Willing is not enough; we must do." He also said, "Whatever you can do or dream, you can begin it. Boldness has genius, power, and magic in it."

We've all heard the expression, "Knowledge is power." But is that really true? Knowledge can't do anything by itself. Only when you act on it will knowledge hold any power for you. Knowledge is fuel, but you still need to start the engine of action.

While we're blowing clichés out of the water, let's take aim at another one: "Be ready when opportunity knocks." But does opportunity really knock? I guarantee you it won't appear at your front door with balloons and a certified check. No bells, no whistles, no fanfare.

Opportunity never knocks, but it's always there—waiting for *you* to knock. It isn't glamorous either. Thomas Edison is one of my heroes, so I quote him often. "Opportunity," he said, "is missed by most people because it's dressed in overalls and looks like work." There's nothing romantic about it.

Make Time for Your Dream

"I'm working a full-time job. I don't like what I'm doing, but there aren't enough hours in the day to pursue my dream too." This is a common complaint, but seldom valid.

According to one recent survey, the average American spends 15 hours a week watching television. Let's say you are like that average American. If you are unhappy with your current career or business choice, begin to restructure your routine by eliminating those 15 hours of tube-time. How many of those hours could you use toward a cherished passion, a "Someday I'll…" goal?

Another source of time is lunch. Fortunately, you can eat and study simultaneously, so five lunch hours each week can be devoted to fulfilling your dream.

Set your alarm clock fifteen minutes earlier than usual, and invest that time in reading a positive book. It can help keep you on track and inspire you to take action. Focus on subject matter associated with what you want to achieve—perhaps a personal or business development book. Do this for a month, until it becomes routine, then set your alarm back another fifteen minutes. Continue this practice over a period of several months until you have a full hour of early morning time devoted to pursuing your goal.

Fifteen hours no longer spent in front of the television, plus five lunch hours, plus seven quiet, early morning hours, gives you a total of 27 hours weekly dedicated to your dream or goal! That's nearly the equivalent of four workdays spent pursuing what you long to do.

Maybe the above scenario seems unrealistic for you, given your personal circumstances. Okay, let's assume that's true. Tell me you cannot find, in your daily schedule, 60 minutes you could be spending more wisely. Locate just 60 minutes, the time it takes to watch one television show. Be honest with yourself. Most of us waste or use poorly at least that much time each day, and usually a lot more.

Take those 60 minutes and reserve them exclusively for your personal and creative development. Guard that time from interruptions and never skip a day, especially if you don't feel like doing it. Dedicate yourself to that time, the same time, every day.

"How much can I possibly get done in 60 minutes?" you may be asking. Perhaps not a lot; however, what could you accomplish with 21,900 minutes, or 365 hours? That string of hours represents 45 eight-hour workdays. This is what one year of following a modest, 60-minute daily schedule gives you. That's plenty of developmental time to help you toward pursuing your dreams and goals. You may not think you're gifted, but you *do* have desire, don't you? So... how strong is it?

Do you commute to and from work? Pop a motivational, personal development, continuing education, or instructional tape or CD into your player and turn your car into a "university on wheels." Absorb creative ideas every day to break your old routine. Listening to a tape or CD every day is a good habit to get into. You'll be using those precious hours to help you become whatever you desire. Listen to them over and over again to be sure you hear and retain what is important to you. It's said that we need to listen to a message at least seven times before we really start to get its full meaning. Wear out those tapes and CDs!

Each of us is an architect. Any worthwhile endeavor begins with the proper planning. Angry, bitter, disillusioned people are often those who see no need for blueprints. They just sort of let things happen, like a ship without a rudder.

While few people are in a position to make an abrupt change in their careers or businesses, it's always possible to make life changes slowly. How many of us can honestly say that 100 percent of a typical day is being used productively? Most of us spend some of our time unwisely. Take those valuable hours and discipline yourself to devote them to the gradual attainment of your desire.

Research, study, and develop a plan whereby you can gradually shift your energies from one career or business to another. Ask for help, as this can be challenging. It requires self-sustaining drive and the desire to stay on course. Ask for support as you need it. Maintain a strong commitment to moving forward. Begin with the assumption that there is always a way, and with persistent focus and effort, you'll eventually find it. If, for some reason, one way doesn't work out, you'll find another.

"Whether you are flying the Atlantic or selling sausages," said Amelia Earhart, "building a skyscraper or driving a truck, your greatest power comes from the fact that you want tremendously to do that very thing, and do it well." So, whatever your goal is—to build a career or business, or something else, it all starts with your desire. That is the gift, pure and simple.

Find a Mentor—*If There's a Shortcut to Success, This Is It*

I was working as a newspaper account executive when I first decided to learn the business side of being an artist. A fellow salesman offered to introduce me to his brother-in-law, Frank Hulick, a full-time professional in the field.

An accomplished wildlife artist, Frank not only took time to critique my artwork and offer encouragement, but also steered me to the best wholesale source for mats, glass, and other art supplies. He shared information about lucrative art shows and festivals, and where to send for applications.

His advice was priceless. By openly sharing this knowledge, Frank made the business of art a less intimidating prospect for me. He really smoothed the road. My goal to be a full-time artist was realized, in no small way, because of Frank's thoughtful assistance. He's a natural mentor. I've spoken with numerous people who feel the same way about him. Frank has helped so many others to fulfill their dreams.

Find a mentor. Seek out people who are successful in your field of interest. Offer to take them to lunch. Be honest. Tell them you need direction, you respect them and what they've accomplished, and could benefit from their expertise. Some will be generous with their wisdom and life experiences. (Though I never invited Frank to lunch, my wife did bake a delicious apple cake for him.) Watch, listen, and learn from them—and do what they did to get where they are.

Be sure to ask these people how they've handled failure and rejection. What would they do differently, given the opportunity to start over? Create a list of such questions before meeting your potential mentors. People enjoy talking about themselves. Listen and learn from what they say to you.

My wife's dream had long been to own and manage a bed-and-breakfast. Jan stayed in many inns before opening one of her own. In those inns, she found many mentors. Once the breakfast dishes were cleared away, most innkeepers were happy to share their personal stories with her.

"What don't you like about this business?" was usually Jan's first question. "Lack of privacy," was a common complaint from innkeepers, and an important factor to keep in mind when searching for an old home with bed-and-breakfast potential. Those gracious innkeepers provided invaluable information, enabling my wife to enter the profession with her eyes wide open. She gained a broad knowledge of the business even before welcoming her first guest.

Be especially courteous to your mentors. When successful people take time from their busy schedules for you, follow up with a note of thanks for their kindness. Show your appreciation.

Feline Wisdom

We live with three cats. In addition to the companionship and affection they provide, these fascinating animals are also good teachers. Cats live wisely. Here are ten lessons you can learn from them:

1. **Begin each day in an upbeat mood.** Cats always get up in a positive frame of mind. They awaken ready to explore the world (or at least their small part of it).
2. **Develop your powers of concentration.** A cat can achieve perfect focus. Watch one when it sights a bird or squirrel. A powerful concentration takes over and the rest of the world disappears.
3. **Be courageous and take a leap.** Cats always jump with confidence. They'll leap distances many times their own height to get to where they want to go.

4. **Occasionally take a detached view.** Cats find a high perch from which to quietly observe their surroundings. People could benefit by doing the same.

5. **See value in imaginative play.** Even a simple piece of string or a paper bag, approached playfully, provides cats great exercise for both mind and body. They use play to "stay loose."

6. **Realize the importance of rest and relaxation.** While I don't recommend their sleep schedule (16 hours a day), cats do know how to relax and find joy in the moment. They handle stress well.

7. **Be patient.** If they wait long enough on a windowsill, cats know that something of interest will come into view.

8. **Clean up after yourself.** We don't need to go into detail about this one. Let's just say that cats take responsibility for their own messes.

9. **Be yourself.** Like people, cats are sometimes slightly zany. (They get that way from living with us!) One moment your cat is sitting quietly on the couch. Suddenly, the fur on its back starts to twitch. The cat stares at you wildly, then darts from the room for no apparent reason. (If you choose to mimic this behavior, do so only around people who know you really well.) Cats accept the streak of irrationality within themselves.

10. **Don't take yourself *too* seriously.** This is the message cats try to convey whenever they roll onto their backs and look at us upside-down. They remind us to lighten up a bit.

"**G**reat perform-
ers don't sit at
the edge of the stage,
their legs dangling, and
drone to the audience
about how wonderful
they are. Take too much
time to get your act to-
gether and you'll be left
on stage in an empty
theatre."

—Bruce Garrabrandt

"**U**nless you were born with a key in your back, don't expect anyone else to wind you up."

—Bruce Garrabrandt

Chapter 4

Exercise Discipline and Persevere

"People become successful often long before their names
or deeds are known. The transformation occurs the moment they
pledge their heart, mind, and spirit, saying,
'I will achieve my dreams.'"
— Bruce Garrabrandt —

One of my favorite quotes is from Henry David Thoreau, and it was easy to memorize. He advised, "Simplify, simplify, simplify."

Life wants to interrupt you sixty times an hour to ask, "Got a minute?" There are many ways the world can distract you. Life has a way of pulling you in a dozen different directions, but only if you let it.

Be determined to stay on track. Concentrate. Practice discipline. Discipline is required for success, and it's deeply intertwined with another essential, perseverance. You need to focus your attention and energies on your desire and stay determined to accomplish your goals. Otherwise, you won't get what you want. It's hard to orchestrate your life if you've scattered your sheet music throughout the theater.

Running to and fro, people often weave and dodge their way around a lot of opportunities. "There's so much I should be doing," they lament, "but I just don't know where to begin." They walk in circles getting nowhere, until their complaint becomes an unwritten epitaph.

Efficient, effective people know a lot of things on their list will never get done—these things just aren't important in the achievement of their goals or dreams. They've learned what to retain and what to eliminate as well as what to delegate.

This kind of streamlined attention brings to mind the artwork of the late Al Hirschfeld, whose delightful drawings chronicled the New York theater scene—and all the performing arts—since the early 1920s. He was a master of the art of caricature.

His witty portraits focused on what was most distinctive about a person—eliminating all unnecessary detail. With just a few, well-placed lines and curves, Hirschfeld not only delineated a performer's likeness, but also defined the heart of that person's character.

His drawings took either hours or days to complete. His theatrical sketches captured a stage filled with movement, and he compressed all that activity onto a sheet of paper. "A magic takes place" is how Hirschfeld described his artistic technique. He became a visual translator of the playwright's intentions, freezing emotion and mood with an economy of line. Simple loops and swirls infused his art with a current of energy. "Mouths became caverns, slits," he said. "Hair might be Brillo, rope, string, thread."

Hirschfeld's imagination cut through the extraneous, leaving only the essence of features and personality. But each remaining line was crucial to the composition. He excelled in the art of simplification. His economy of line produced drawings full of playful humor. I always smile when I see one.

Take what Al Hirschfeld did with his pen and apply it to your personal goals. You write your own script in life, and the greatest fulfillment comes to those who practice good editing. As bestselling author Mario Puzo said, "The secret to writing is rewriting."

You can't sign up for every course of interest when your life lasts only one semester. Pick and choose carefully.

Keep Hirschfeld's drawings in mind. Cut through extraneous details. Simplify and focus on what's essential to cultivating your own gift—your desire.

Success Is Found in Overcoming Challenges

Here's another favorite Thoreau quote of mine. "If one advances confidently in the direction of his dreams and endeavors to live the life which he has imagined, he will meet with a success unexpected in common hours."

Being confident and optimistic about your dreams is effortless when your life is going well and you see tangible evidence of progress toward a goal. At these times, faith in yourself is as natural as blinking and breathing.

The real test comes if you run into some major obstacles and no one is there who believes in you and what you're doing. Even your dog seems aloof.

If such periods of time come, and they may, your confidence and faith are given an opportunity to become more than mere words that make you feel warm and cozy. They can support and guide you, pushing you forward, defining both your character and the substance of your desire.

Football coach Vince Lombardi said, "It's easy to have faith in yourself and have discipline when you're a winner, when you're number one. What you've got to have is faith and discipline when you're *not* a winner."

Success is in the challenge. "Lasting accomplishment," said actress Helen Hayes, "is achieved through a long, slow climb and self-discipline." Successful people often say jokingly that it takes 15 years to become an overnight success.

As discussed earlier, we are born to believe in ourselves and have faith that our lives hold purpose. Otherwise, we disparage the greatest of gifts.

If you don't experience more challenges than comforts in life, you're not really stretching and growing. Genius is usually the romantic name we give to thoughtful endurance.

If things always came up smelling like roses, the scent would soon go unnoticed. People usually take for granted whatever comes to them easily. It's our hard (and hopefully smart) work and challenges that give us a true appreciation for what we've earned. They bring value to our goals. Since challenges met and overcome only strengthen us, why not welcome them? We do want to grow stronger, don't we?

Learning how to lift the weight of challenges from our shoulders tones and develops who we are. Think of challenges as exercise equipment for the mind. Obstacles are an integral part of any life well spent.

Wherever you live, Challenge may always be the neighbor who stops in without phoning first. Open the door for him. To pretend you're not home is to choose not to grow and therefore not to achieve your goals and dreams. The greatest natural resource available to you is the power of your mind to overcome life's challenges. That which is best within you can be discovered and mined in no other way.

"The great crisis must come," said Theodore Roosevelt, "or no man has the chance to develop great qualities."

You're Fired!

Several years ago, radio talk-show host Rush Limbaugh opened his phone lines to people who had been forced to change careers in mid-life. He wanted to hear how they had used this challenging event as a springboard to greater success. Limbaugh thought it was crucial to provide listeners with a positive alternative to the whining victims continually presented to us by the mainstream media. America, argued Limbaugh, was still the best place to fulfill a dream, and he wanted his callers to prove it.

What followed was the most inspiring three hours of radio I've ever heard. People phoned in with incredible stories of personal setbacks. Some detailed painful hardships and slow progress in putting their lives back together and moving forward. Many callers had become entrepreneurs, using the experience of sudden job loss as an opportunity to strike out on their own.

It hadn't been easy for any of them. But their sense of accomplishment and positive attitude in recounting these challenges were evident, and truly impressive! With enthusiasm, they spoke of their achievements, thankful for the crises which had challenged them to stretch and grow.

Most of these callers to Limbaugh's program were not only survivors, but had gone on to achieve an even greater degree of success and fulfillment. Faced with challenges, motivated people build their own mental bleachers, filling the stands with cheering thoughts that spur them on to win their dreams.

The Secret to Happiness

Reporter John Stossel explored the subject of happiness in an excellent television special.

He interviewed a young man who had sustained serious injuries in an automobile collision. He had been left as a quadriplegic. One year had passed.

The quadriplegic had faced his physical challenges with a positive spirit, using what most people would call a tragedy as an opportunity to change careers. He was now a teacher. His disability hadn't kept him from gaining a new sense of purpose in life. Satisfaction from helping others brought him even greater fulfillment.

Stossel's report concluded that genuine happiness is usually linked to having a worthwhile purpose.

Transforming Tragedy into Talent

Occasionally, I exhibit at art shows with an exceptional artist named Eric. His story is also an inspiring one.

While driving home from the beach one summer afternoon in 1963, Eric was nearly killed when another car slammed into his Volkswagen Beetle. At 17, he suddenly found himself a quadriplegic.

Doctors told Eric he would never walk again. He refused to believe them. But, after a year with no improvement, the grim truth of his condition hit Eric hard. Reality crushed his spirit. He spent the next year filled with anger and bitterness. Friends eventually stopped visiting him.

Finally, Eric's mother gave him an ultimatum, "Either do something with your life, or go into a nursing home. You're not going to stay here and feel sorry for yourself."

Her words were spoken out of tough love, and fortunately they reached Eric. He chose to turn his attitude around. He took positive action. Holding a paintbrush between his teeth, Eric mustered his desire and painstakingly trained himself to be an artist.

It took many months of determined practice, but Eric's efforts eventually bore creative fruit. His artwork became good enough to sell. He perfected an artistic technique which he launched into a full-time, profitable career.

Today, Eric is part of a cottage industry. He employs a number of people to frame and market his fine work, and to manage the financial side of his business.

At the time of his collision, Eric's doctors predicted that he'd live only 15 to 20 years. That was 40 years ago. He continues to work daily, spending 7½ hours in his wheelchair, paintbrush between his teeth, producing art. His life is filled with purpose. Long ago, he chose to meet his personal challenges with grace and grit. By doing so, Eric brought forth an abiding skill he can share with thousands of others.

Thought Versus Feeling

A few people think things through; the rest only think they do. Not many people trudge up the stairs of thought. Most glide along on escalators of feeling. "I don't feel like doing that." Sounds familiar, doesn't it? For many of us, it becomes a motivating force in our lives. We're disciples of impulse.

It's far easier to follow your feelings than it is to command your thoughts. But it's best not to allow just your emotions to guide you. Follow your heart, but back up your feelings with sound judgment. Where feelings rule, rational thought is in exile. You still need to think things through.

On days when I don't feel like sitting at my easel to draw, and they are many, I park myself in front of it for several hours anyway. Some days are productive, others are not; but I'm there at the same time, daily. It's worth it.

The choice to override emotional impulse with mental diligence will eventually pay big dividends for you too.

Professional writers stress the importance of disciplined routine in their work. Empty sheets of paper, or a blank computer screen, can be daunting to a writer, but feelings of dread are shoved aside through discipline. The number of pages written daily may be zero or 20, good or bad, but, nonetheless, writers sit every day for the allotted time, and write until they reach their self-imposed deadline.

Establish a routine for yourself and stay with it. Feelings will always float through the ballroom of your mind, but you don't have to dance with them.

Make every decision in the house of reason. Keep emotion outside, even when it presses its nose against the window and begs to come in. Remain with the rhythm of your routine. It's generally not smart to take action solely based on your feelings. View feelings as "a call to thought" for you.

Prune Your Dead Branches

In our backyard stands a century-old maple tree we call the Grand Old Lady. Dead branches were carefully trimmed away some years ago to improve her health and form.

In summer, the maple is lush with foliage, and our Grand Old Lady greets the autumn dressed in brilliant yellow-gold. Even the winter months find her looking majestic, strong winds having little effect on her sturdy branches. Pruning has strengthened and enhanced this lovely old tree.

How much dead wood do people carry around? Useless branches can often be seen everywhere. Debilitating and unattractive, they need to be cut from our lives. Rid yourself of any self-doubt, laziness, procrastination, fear, discouragement, guilt, negativity, regret, ignorance, blame, resentment, irresponsibility, worry, rationalization, and pretense you may have.

Trimming away these and other dead branches strengthens, forces, and directs your energies in positive, healthy ways. Pruning is a powerful and necessary tool for personal growth. It fosters the development of your potential.

Slow Down, Simplify and—*See*

By slowing down we can hasten our education. For example, Amish children cannot join the church until they become adults, usually between the ages of 18 and 22. Prior to that, they often manage to get a taste of the outside world. Occasionally, rock music from a boom box is heard blaring inside a horse-drawn buggy. Adolescent boys have been known to visit pool halls, drive cars, and sample alcoholic beverages. Despite these and other worldly temptations, 80 percent of Amish youth go on to join the church and choose to stay within the community.

Visitors to our inn are sometimes surprised to hear this. "That's a high percentage," a guest might say. "You'd think it would be hard for Amish kids to give up everything the modern world has to offer."

The Amish are, by and large, a wise group of people. They've boiled life down to its essentials. The quiet, uncluttered lifestyle they practice keeps their community in constant touch with the natural world, in tune with the deeper, natural rhythms of daily life. "Simplified but intense" might be a good way to describe the Amish culture.

All of us could benefit from this approach to living. You needn't sell your car, buy a horse, and grow a beard. Don't alter your attire or mode of transportation; just change your pace. In the rush to make ends meet and keep up with life's activities, we may be quick to lose sight of ourselves and our purpose. Learn to slow down and practice a silent observation of your world. Insight comes when we quiet our minds. It is inner vision. It is learning to see and understand on a more profound, expansive level.

Emily Dickinson was one of this country's greatest poets. She seldom left her home in Amherst, Massachusetts. Within the uncomplicated world of that house and an outside garden, she discovered the special quality which life holds even in its simplest forms.

Emily Dickinson's intense power of observation was transformed into hundreds of short poems, created in easy words, but containing profound meaning. The poet narrowed the parameters of her physical world, broadened her inner vision, and saw life more clearly.

Listen intently, amid the world's noise, and you will always hear music.

My innkeeper-wife is an artist in our kitchen. She loves to cook. I watch her create delicious broths and sauces by reducing them over high heat—boiling the liquids down to half their original volume. This greatly intensifies the flavor of what remains in the pot.

In the noisy chaos of daily life (for most of us, anyway), we need to engage in our own form of reduction. We can do this by rising early each morning to spend some time in silent solitude. Treasure these moments by using them for reading a positive book or planning your day.

Hauling yourself out of a warm bed earlier than necessary is a ritual that requires tenacity. You may be resistant to the idea in the beginning. I understand those feelings. I've had them myself. But this disciplined action, arduous at first, will soon open your mind to fresh perspectives and insights. You'll carry them with you the rest of your day and on into the rest of your life. As they guide you to discern what is essential and good, your life will intensify in joyful discovery.

Time with Yourself Sets the Stage for Your Day

Though I'm going to repeat myself, it's not a sign of early senility. The last two paragraphs need emphasis. A stronger, more creative you cannot be formed in the thick of the daily routine. The frenzied swirl of others' demands, expectations, and negative opinions makes that virtually impossible.

Step out of the world and into your life. Stake your claim to 60 minutes of daily, personal, goal-oriented time, and defend it against all intrusions. This time with yourself is essential to live deeply in the world without being consumed by it.

Rub the sleep from your eyes tomorrow morning and awaken to new possibilities. In time, you'll become well acquainted with your potential. An inner calm awaits you, designed to keep you in mental balance between your need for personal growth and life's demands on your time and energy.

Would you like to follow, as Henry David Thoreau would say, "the beat of a different drummer"? How about carrying your own drum instead? This is what ritual solitude can help you do. Distance yourself from the world in early morning to cultivate your gift of desire.

Process and the Goal

Most diets fail, even when people succeed in taking off excess weight. During weeks or months of sacrifice and denial, dieters long for the day when they'll be thin again and able to eat, in moderation, all the foods they enjoy. Unfortunately, their moderation approach seldom works in the long-term because their old habits haven't changed. So the surplus poundage slowly (and sometimes quickly) returns.

The key to losing weight and keeping it off is to abandon the idea of dieting altogether. Sustained weight loss is achieved only by altering the way in which we view food. Any drastic but temporary change in our eating habits, to reach some ideal goal, will ultimately fail. The healthy food choices you make, and whatever portions you need to eat in order to keep an ideal weight, need to become a permanent part of your daily life.

"In my world there is no such thing as a potato," said comedian Sid Caesar. A beefy man during his television heyday in the 1950s, Caesar managed to stay thin for four decades. He and other successful "dieters," for lack of a better word, focus on the process and the goal. First they decide where they want to be weight-wise. Then they devise or follow an eating and exercise plan to lose the excess weight and maintain their new weight for the rest of their lives. These people approach weight loss with the understanding that modest, permanent changes are much preferred to severe, short-term ones.

This dedication to goal and process is applicable to any passionate endeavor. It's important to focus on a desired outcome or you'll be aimless in your pursuit—a wandering generality! You need to follow your dream, whatever it is. However, you also need to find pleasure in your daily actions by working creatively and loving what you do. Then you can know fulfillment all along the way to your goal. Joy in the process of doing brings satisfaction and bolsters you during moments of failure. Look at them as learning experiences in the pursuit of your dreams.

Resilience comes to those who keep their eyes on their goal and dedicate themselves to the doing. Our real joy in life needs to be discovered during those long stretches of time between moments of achievement. The journey is the success—a *progressive* realization of a worthwhile goal or dream.

Some Facts About the Rich

One of my pet peeves is the mistaken belief that the ability to succeed is determined by how much money someone has. We may look at affluent people and think they had an easier time of it, or an unfair advantage. There's a lot of class envy in society, and much of it is misguided.

Let me give you a few facts about the rich among us, culled from Thomas J. Stanley's book, *The Millionaire Next Door*. Eighty percent of millionaires in America are first-generation wealthy. Nothing was given to them—they earned it. To look at these people, you'd never know they were rich. Many of the wealthy among us actually live in middle-class neighborhoods. Usually married only once, they are frugal people and great savers. They hold traditional values. Who are they? The majority are dry cleaners, bowling alley owners, scrap metal haulers, and small business owners—not doctors or lawyers.

Most millionaires have a strong belief in themselves and a dedication to their dreams. Their wealth was accumulated slowly, steadily, and with patience. Money didn't fall into their laps.

We need to discard the myth that most wealthy people are evil exploiters of the working people. The rich *are* hard working, dedicated people who also are persistent and work smart. When they achieve financial freedom they usually continue working because they enjoy being productive. When you know these facts, you understand what separates the rich from average-thinking people. It's not class or money—it's action, discipline, and perseverance. These are people who use the life of their desire so they can live their dreams. Your recognition of this is the first step toward becoming one of them.

You don't need money to be successful—you need to be successful to have money! It is the result of being progressively successful, which is driven by your desire.

Don't Let Gossip Distract You

People love to gossip. In business offices, places of worship, and neighborhoods, gossip is a shortcut many of us take to feel good about ourselves.

It's impossible to gain genuine self-improvement when we sit back and gleefully tear down the people around us. Gossip is convenient. It's a tempting, titillating, easy habit to slip into. Chattering about the faults and flawed behaviors of others puffs us up with a feeling of superiority. But what does it accomplish? What success does it lead to? None.

Not only is gossip not helpful, it is both hurtful and devious. It corrodes character. The false sense of superiority gossip gives us masks our personal shortcomings and distracts us from the disciplined work we need to be doing to better ourselves and our lives.

Growing up, I remember my dad liked to recite these words about gossip from Robert Louis Stevenson: "There is so much good in the worst of us, and so much bad in the best of us, that it behooves all of us not to talk about the rest of us." Gossiping is a poor use of valuable time. Instead of talking about others, become someone others will rave about and emulate.

Think of friends, relatives, and coworkers you know who like to gossip. They spend so much time each day finding fault instead of looking for the good in people around them. Why do they do that? What is it about some people that compels them to tear others down?

I'm no Rhodes Scholar, but I do know that people who genuinely like themselves, those who have a passion for excellence and keep a positive attitude, seldom feel the need to gossip. They don't look for flaws in others in order to feel better about themselves. Negativity gets you nowhere.

Associate only with positive-thinking people who live each day with quiet self-confidence and a kind word for others. Such people are following their dreams and making a difference in the world.

Preparation and Patience

If success were a freshly painted old house, some people would stand across the street from it and say, "Sure, that house looks great. It's easy when you have the right brushes, a ladder, and enough paint to get the job done."

What goes unappreciated by these admirers is the tedious preparation necessary for the painting to take place; many hours of careful scraping, sanding, and patching were spent to ensure that the project would be beautifully done. The wood also had to be primed before the finish coats were applied. To bypass this work and just slap on a coat or two would soon result in a house with its paint cracked, blistered, and peeling away from the wood.

When we stand across the street from success, it's fine to be dazzled by the attractive results, but we also need to appreciate the time involved in doing the job properly. Keep in mind the patient preparation required to achieve any worthwhile goal.

Some of us may like to fantasize that our life should be like a movie. We may envision ourselves becoming a success, conveniently suffering and overcoming all the frustrations and awkward stumblings of a lifetime within a neat two-hour period.

How romantic and exciting the pursuit of a goal would be if we could just condense and tighten our experiences. Wouldn't it be nice to live only those events which propel us forward to fulfill our dream, in just one sitting? Why not throw in some popcorn while you're at it?

When it doesn't come easily, people often don't want to make the effort. That's why most people live average, routine lives—they don't want to bother with anything beyond the grind they're in. They don't like what they're doing, yet refuse to change. Face it, there are often many obstacles to overcome in the process of getting where we truly long to be. But challenges in the pursuit of what we love—our dream—are bearable. They're just part of the necessary process. Our desire, when strong enough, will help to sustain us.

Grandmother liked to say, "Honey, put one foot in front of the other and keep moving forward." Widowed at age 50, in 1952, she was left to fend for herself at a time when women were largely dependent upon their husbands for economic survival. Grandma Horner, a woman of great determination, slowly acquired the skills of an astute businesswoman. She involved herself in the community, joining a variety of charitable organizations. Her perseverance through painful loss strengthened her self-confidence and enriched her life.

Long-term success cannot be like a snapshot, achieved with the clicking of a shutter. Such success is a jigsaw-puzzle photograph, created bit by bit, with patience and persistence, until all the pieces are in place.

Do not demand perfection from yourself. Locate perfection on the map, then set out on foot to get there, visiting as many educational sites as possible along the way. But don't ever expect to arrive at perfection. Instead, strive for excellence. Develop patience. It usually takes a long time to become really accomplished. Long-term success requires long-term commitment.

My first drawings looked terrible. Slowly, over a period of several years, I began to see improvement. Fortunately, I understood early that you don't need to be good to be an artist; you just need to want to be good and keep working at it.

Don't expect to be an instant success. Give yourself time to grow and succeed. Nurture your dream. Again, it's best not to compare yourself to others more accomplished than you are. That wouldn't be fair to you. Your task is to focus on your own progress.

Creating a detailed drawing teaches patience. Some of my pieces take more than 300 hours to complete. You learn, as an artist, to think incrementally. To sit in front of a blank sheet of paper and envision a completed drawing can be quite intimidating, so I never do that. My goal, a finished work of art, is broken into many smaller goals, painstaking steps made slowly with determination, that eventually take me to where I want to be.

For writers, it isn't a book or an article they write, it's one word at a time. For composers, one note, then another, and another. Creativity isn't a product. It's an incremental process, a way of doing things. (Be sure to set incremental goals, but not so high that you dislocate a shoulder in your stretch to reach them.)

It's always easier for us just to think of the future than it is to act in the present to create the future we really want. Many are in love with the idea of being artists, writers, composers, actors, business owners, and such. Many people romanticize and fantasize about what it must be like, but they never get around to the practicality of actually doing and experiencing. Whatever you want to do well will most likely require much practice and learning. Leave your frustration at the door and find joy in the process. Don't take yourself too seriously—have fun with it!

A Big Task Broken Down into Smaller Increments Is Doable

Jane Taylor, a British writer of juvenile fiction in the early 19th Century, told a fable about an old kitchen clock with a pendulum that suddenly decided to stop moving.

"I'm tired of ticking," the pendulum tells the face of the clock. "I happened, this morning, to be calculating how many times I would have to tick in the course of only the next 24 hours." The thought of ticking 86,400 times a day had exhausted it, so the pendulum quit. Multiplying those strokes by the number of weeks and months in a year only increased the pendulum's discouragement.

The face of the clock listened to the pendulum's complaint, then calmly asked him to tick just six more times. This the pendulum did, after which the face asked, "Was that at all fatiguing?"

"Not in the least," said the pendulum. "It's not of six strokes that I complain, nor of sixty, but of millions."

The face tells the pendulum to keep in mind that, although it can think of a million strokes in an instant, it only needs to tick once in any given moment. It just needs to focus on "the present moment in which it needs to swing."

Viewed in this way, the pendulum sees its task as no longer overwhelming, and it resumes ticking as loud as ever.

Cultivate Restless Patience

Necessity may be the mother of Invention, but its father is always Restlessness. Cultivate a restless patience. Carefully structure each day, devoting time daily toward the achievement of your dream. In this way you build a small fire within yourself. You become eager for accomplishment.

Accept that, in moving forward, you'll be taking one step at a time. This can be challenging but you can do it. On some days your pace will be brisk—you may break into a run—while on other days, you may only take a measured step or two. At times you'll find yourself standing still, in need of encouragement. This is natural. Remain focused and disciplined, knowing that doubt and frustration are ever present, ready to thwart your efforts. But you can overcome these foes of success by your faith and determination.

Wanting to leapfrog over obstacles and get to where you want to be is normal, but you need to temper restlessness with patience. Concentrate on maintaining forward momentum. Balance the full scope of your journey, keeping the big picture in mind, with an acceptance that many individual steps are required on the path you've chosen. Live in each step with a self-engendered enthusiasm. It's an inside job. Walk, sprint, tumble, leap, or crawl—but remain steadily on that path. Fill yourself with restless patience. A continual moving forward by inches will put you miles ahead of most people because they are stuck in a rut rather than on track to their dreams.

Remember to be flexible. Remain solid of purpose, but keep fluid the means to achieve it. To fulfill a dream, it isn't enough to just push forward. You also need to know when to jump back, skip sideways, or pause to do an occasional headstand on your path. When you are pushing forward, don't just push hard. Push thoughtfully.

Passion with Patient Perseverance Creates Talent

"This carpet has to go," said my wife, shortly after moving into our home. The wall-to-wall carpeting throughout our house, originally harvest gold, was later dyed an apple green. Now, after 20 years, its blonde roots were again showing through in spots.

We decided to tear all the carpeting out, hoping to restore our home's original 1853 floors. That would depend, of course, on the condition of the wood.

Careful chiseling and prying away of the sub-flooring exposed random-width planks of pine and fir. They looked to be in pretty good shape. Since I do a poor impression of Bob Vila, the host of the popular TV show *This Old House,* we hired professionals to sand and finish the floors. Jeff and Carey Hoover are brothers whose reputation for fine restoration work is well-known in our area. Jeff, the older one, gave us a good history lesson about our floors, telling us, "The wood used here came from trees more than a century old when they were cut down 150 years ago. The logs were first floated in the river, or else put into a holding pool of cold water. That forced the sap deep into the wood."

"Why was that done?" I asked.

"Think of it as an early form of pressure-treating," Jeff said. "It preserved the wood. When we sand your floors today, 150 years later, we can still smell sap!"

Jeff has great respect for the quality of materials used in the past. "We'll go to some of these old farmhouses in the area and find bare windowsills. No paint on them for thirty years or more. We just sand a little, then prime and paint, and the sills are as good as new. You couldn't do that with today's wood."

"Why not?" I asked.

"Mature trees, the kind used to build your home, were slow growing. That makes for sturdy wood. After so many years, the tree's rings are very close together. The wood is dense, and more durable."

Jeff thinks people move too fast today. "Time is our enemy now," he told me. "Technology wows us with its speed, but we lose so much in the process. Trees are force-grown and harvested quickly. They're cut younger, so the rings are spread out. The wood lacks density.

"Latent sap gives wood its long life, but logs are no longer put into cold water. Now they're kiln-dried. Today's wood has no life to it. It begins to rot from the inside, even on expensive new houses." Jeff shook his head sadly. "We've sacrificed quality for speed," he said.

Jeff's observations about the quality of wood also apply to the quality of people's lives. Most of us, to some degree, sacrifice quality for speed. Ours is a society where too many expect the instant gratification of their desires. What they want, they want *now*.

But things of substance and value take time to develop. Excellence can't be rushed into being by the strength of desire alone. Passion without patience has no real life to it, and many goals soon rot from the inside. Discipline yourself to work and wait. Passion and patient perseverance are not substitutes for talent—they are parents of it—that from which talents are spawn. Slow your mind to a realistic speed while you're in pursuit of any meaningful endeavor. Time becomes your most valuable partner once you learn to work at its methodical pace. Patience and persistence, i.e., wholehearted dedication, hold a quiet power.

Gigantic inflexible aspirations, not broken down into reasonable chunks, seldom rise very high. Ambitions built slowly, brick by brick, goal by goal, are best. "Great things are not done by impulse," wrote Vincent van Gogh, "but by a series of small things brought together."

Blunders, Bungles, and Boners—*Oh My!*

We're always going to make mistakes. Just accept the fact and keep moving. Television weather forecasters do it with ease. They tell us to "expect a sunny day tomorrow," and we wake up to rain. They warn that "a blizzard is on its way," and everyone hurries to the supermarket for toilet paper and milk. But not a flake falls.

How do TV weather people react to these inaccuracies? They smile, shrug their shoulders, and proceed to give you the best five-day forecast they can. They don't expect to always be right. We enjoy poking fun at them with comments like, "In what other profession could you be so consistently wrong and still keep your job?"

The truth is, weather forecasters are usually correct. It's just easy for us to target them for their mistakes. We do the same thing to ourselves. We dwell on personal blunders, bungles, and boners, beating ourselves up over errors in judgment, as if progress were possible without them! This self-torture often inhibits us from going forward.

Let's take a lesson from TV weather people. We need to realize that outside forces and our own mistakes may trip us up occasionally. Goof-ups may make us look silly, but what looks sillier is our unwillingness to smile, shrug our shoulders, and move on with confidence.

Gifts Are the Result of Diligent Work—*Not Birth*

John is a successful nature photographer. People who admire his wildlife studies and majestic landscapes sometimes ask him, "Is this a gift, or are you self-taught?"

"This is a gift I got for Christmas one year," he tells them, his eyes twinkling. After taking a moment to enjoy their puzzled reaction, he goes on to explain the creative process used in his work. "First, I develop the idea for a photograph. I picture in my mind the scene I want to capture on film. Then I pack up and go to that part of the country where I'm most likely to get it."

Some people think wildlife photography is the result of sitting quietly in the woods, waiting for something to happen. "I wish it were that easy," says John. "The way I work is to single out an animal and study it, learning its habits and routine. Then I endeavor to make the photographic image I have in my mind happen. The process can take ten days or more, and many times I don't get the shot I want."

John is a good-natured, patient man, with dogged persistence. "If I quit at that point, I'd be a failure as a nature photographer," he says. "I keep going back to the same area, sometimes many trips over a period of two or three years, until I come home with the photograph I want."

In addition to a fine eye and good sense of composition, John possesses a strong background in animal research and a broad geographical knowledge. He knows every part of the U.S., and the animals which inhabit it, through years of painstaking study and travel.

"I've been chased by all kinds of critters," John told me. He has shinnied up countless trees to avoid angry bull elk, was knocked down by a grizzly, and routinely faces threats from a host of other animals.

It requires far more than the clicking of a shutter to capture John's beautiful photographs. It takes decades of determined preparation, practice, and perseverance. Excellence always takes time.

When Desire Is Strong Enough, Success Can Be Achieved— *Under All Kinds of Circumstances*

If you fail to reach a goal, it doesn't mean you're a failure. You just learned what doesn't work for you. You may need to take a different approach.

Franklin Delano Roosevelt was stricken with polio at age 39 and lost the use of his legs. His goal was to walk again. He was determined to find some procedure, therapy, or exercise that would produce a cure. He never did.

I guess you could say that, in one sense, FDR failed. He didn't get the result he was looking for in that area of his life. But look at the bigger picture. His boundless enthusiasm and determination didn't give him back his legs. Instead, they gave him the Presidency of the United States. His positive spirit and tenacity stirred a nation in the depths of its Depression. He gave people hope when they desperately needed it. You needn't agree with FDR's politics to appreciate his undying optimism. He had the right personality to see a nation through the Depression and World War II.

I wonder if Roosevelt would have become President had he not lost the use of his legs. That challenge brought out the best in him. His courageous spirit served him well, taking him to the pinnacle of political achievement.

For every failed effort you point to, I can show you others who faced greater obstacles, tougher circumstances, and more devastating setbacks, yet managed to overcome them all to achieve their desires.

There's great danger in believing that some people are destined to fail, no matter what they do. When the going gets tough and the frustration level grows, you may also believe that you are one of those people for whom failure is just inevitable. That losing attitude would be a self-fulfilling prophecy. Refuse to accept failure as a final condition in life. In your effort to succeed, you, like FDR, might not get exactly what you want, but you may get more than you dreamed possible.

Stop Trying and—*Start Doing*

We're more likely to succeed in life if we never try to reach a goal.

How's that again?

We can't *try* to do anything. "Your own resolution to succeed," Lincoln said, "is more important than any other one thing." To be resolved is to be committed. We'll either do something, however long that may take, or we won't. When we "try" to accomplish a goal, what we're implicitly saying is, "Well, I may not reach this goal, despite my efforts."

Listen to cigarette smokers who say "I've tried to quit." But what does that really mean? They stopped smoking until their discomfort level grew too high, at which point they returned to the habit. When you've truly resolved to quit smoking and nicotine withdrawal begins, you don't light up. You persevere through the pain because you're committed to your decision to stop smoking. As soon as you do that, you've joined the ranks of the non-smokers.

The same is true for dieters and alcoholics, and anyone else who chooses to make a positive, permanent change in his or her life. It's challenging, and it takes a total commitment. If you say, "I'll try," you give yourself an out. Erase "try" from your vocabulary and substitute with the words, "I'm doing it."

Be a Darned Fool—*You'll Love the Results*

Comedian W.C. Fields used to jokingly say, "If at first you don't succeed, try, try again—and then quit. No sense being a darned fool about it." Fields obviously never applied this "only for laughs" advice to his own life. As a young boy, he longed to become a great juggler, so he practiced tirelessly, obsessed with the desire to juggle. At times, he could be found crying in frustration, but he simply would not quit. He remained a darned fool about it. He wasn't gifted, but he had desire. He did it wrong until he got it right.

Fields learned to juggle, all right. He juggled his way right into vaudeville, performing in top theaters around the world. Later, he juggled his way into the movies and comedy history. He took juggling routines to his grave that have never been duplicated.

Whatever you desire to do, always be a darned fool about it, and never let failure get you down. Mickey Rooney says, "You always pass failure on the way to success." He was in the position to know. His life was a roller coaster of ups and downs, but, through it all, he persevered.

"Never confuse a single defeat with a final defeat." That's great advice from writer F. Scott Fitzgerald.

You can either sink in the mud of frustration or slog through it and get to the other side. People who win are, in reality, soldiers in boot camp. But picture them marching in a parade with music playing, banners flying, and medals glimmering on their chests.

Successful people have fallen more often than the rest of humanity. They've just refused to *stay* down. They continue to pick themselves up, always doing their best to follow their dreams and make a difference.

Sightless, Soundless Vision—*A Gift Beyond Compare*

"We can do anything we want to do if we stick to it long enough." Do you know who said that? Helen Keller. As a young girl, she faced obstacles to success almost too horrendous to contemplate. How do you learn to speak, read, or reason, when your eyes can't see and your ears can't hear? How do you begin to communicate with the outside world when your inner world is silent darkness?

Thanks to Annie Sullivan, a wonderful teacher and friend, Helen Keller came to understand that, despite her severe physical limitations, she, too, possessed abundant potential. She grew to become an inspirational example of successful living for people throughout the world. The woman literally walked with kings. "Life is either a daring adventure," she wrote, "or nothing."

If Helen Keller could accomplish this with no functional eyes or ears, imagine what you could do with *your* life! Next time you feel like the odds are against you, think of Helen Keller and remember her words: "We can do anything we want to do if we stick to it long enough." Don't make excuses. Look at handicaps, disadvantages, and challenges as gifts that spur your desire to overcome them and excel.

Perfect Circles

It's impossible to draw a perfect circle, right? Let me tell you about my eighth-grade science teacher. It was his first year of teaching, and I remember he talked a lot about the planets, drawing them as circles on the blackboard. From September to June, he drew his planets so many times that, by the end of the school year, he was drawing nearly flawless circles. Do anything long enough and you're going to get good at it.

The Freedom to Be Great—*By Duplicating the Great*

I've learned that you can go wherever you choose in life, but only you can get yourself there. That doesn't mean you have to go it alone. The wisest consultants in the world, living or not, continue to serve us and are reached by reading a book. Study their lives. Absorb the richness of knowledge and insight they have to offer. Ask your mentor or leader to recommend some books to you.

One of my favorite consultants is Frederick Douglass. He was born a slave in 19th Century America. As a boy, Douglass knew he possessed the potential for greatness, born in every human being. Imagine how trapped he must have felt, denied the freedom to realize his potential.

Well, the slaveowner's wife showed compassion for young Frederick and began teaching him how to read. When her husband discovered what she was doing, he quickly put an end to it. But then it was too late. Learning to read had become an obsession with Douglass. Even at his young age, he knew that education and dedicated work would be his ticket to freedom and success.

He managed to get his hands on a book of great world speeches. Douglass not only learned how to read that book, he committed it to memory. That's how hungry he was to better himself. Just think: Memorize the world's greatest speeches and you also learn how to organize your thoughts, how to reason, and how to persuade others.

Douglass kept his growing knowledge hidden, biding his time until he could make his escape to freedom. He endured the indignities and occasional lashings—the unfair treatment given him by ignorant men. Eventually, he did escape to the North, becoming the most eloquent spokesman for the black cause in 19th Century America. Lincoln would refer to him as "my friend, Douglass."

Now, if Frederick Douglass could rise above such bleak circumstances to fulfill his dreams, what excuse could we possibly have for not succeeding in life? *Excuses are self-injected embalming fluid.*

Both Frederick Douglass and Helen Keller were created from the same materials used to make you and me. Their gift was their unstoppable desire to succeed. That's a choice available to all of us.

Enlist for the long haul when you honestly want to earn the rank of "Successful."

Fat Man with a Lisp—*Desire Turned His Challenge into a Gift*

"Never give in, never. Never, never. Never..."

When his facial features were compared with those of a bulldog, Winston Churchill was pleased. He noted that the bulldog's nose was short and slanted backward. In this way, he said, the dog could continue to breathe without letting go of his prey.

Churchill never let go. His tenacity made him one of the most beloved and important figures of the 20th Century. Without that bulldog trait, he would have never made it into the history books.

In childhood, Churchill was lonely and shy. His parents were preoccupied with their busy social lives and virtually ignored him. Raised by a nanny and sent away to school at age seven, Churchill began exhibiting bulldog tendencies in his teens. Suffering from a pronounced stutter and lisp, he dealt with both by joining a debate society, where he soon overcame these challenges and flourished.

As a young man, he served in the military, published books, and later was elected to the British Parliament. By the late 1920s, however, his political career appeared to be over. Voted out in 1929, at age 55, he was seen as washed up and over the hill. Churchill spent the 1930s nearly forgotten. But he focused on his career as an author, and never stopped writing. For almost a decade he warned Britain and the world about a man named Adolph Hitler. With great foresight, he described what would happen if Europe failed to prepare an adequate military defense. No one listened to him. He was an old man whose relevance had seemingly passed.

Like the bulldog, Churchill kept breathing and wouldn't let go. He continued to make accurate predictions about Germany's expansionist plans and, when Hitler's troops began to march across Europe, Churchill's call to re-arm was remembered. The British elected him Prime Minister. At 66, the washed-up, old man was suddenly an inspirational leader who rallied his people and guided them through their darkest days.

"Never give in, never. Never, never. Never..." Inspiration dawns only on those who stay awake to prepare for its arrival.

Success can be found in any failure when you commit to moving ahead. If you don't fall apart when your plans do, a large measure of success is already yours. Each failure is another step forward. Defeat conquers only those who sit down and give up the quest.

So long as your heart keeps beating and you keep going, you'll experience no real dead ends in life.

Four Stories of Uncommon Discipline, Perseverance, and Desire

Winners in gambling casinos exert a strong influence on the people around them. You stand at a slot machine, feeding it quarters and pulling the lever, just to have your change disappear. Meanwhile, the guy to your left keeps hitting winning combinations. Bells are ringing. Quarters gush from his machine. You glance to your right, just in time to see a woman win the jackpot. She's jumping up and down. Your slot-machine neighbors don't look any smarter than you, but *they're* winning! So you continue to drop quarters, five at a time now, into your machine. The infectious effect of seeing others hit the jackpot spurs you on to also become a winner.

In casinos, it's only the management which ultimately becomes successful. But the psychological principle at work there can be used to make you a *real* winner in life. When we acquaint ourselves with those who overcame tough obstacles to achieve their dreams, as in the following four examples, their stories can inspire and sustain our own motivation to succeed.

1. Nice Girls Didn't—*But She Had Desire.* At age 25, Florence Nightingale decided to dedicate her life to a career in nursing. Her parents were horrified. As affluent people, they thought it was disgraceful that their daughter would choose such a lowly profession.

In 1845, hospitals were crowded, unsanitary places. The stench of them made visitors nauseated. Nurses were often drunk and of low character. Sometimes a nurse would supplement her meager income by turning to prostitution.

In short, "Nice girls didn't." Eight years would pass before Florence Nightingale could openly pursue her dream. She was more than a little depressed when she said, "No advantage that I can see comes of my living on. I shall never do anything and am worse than dust and nothing…. Oh, for some strong thing to sweep this loathsome life into the past."

Florence remained the dutiful daughter at home with her parents. But the fire of desire was within her, and not even depression could put it out. She rose each morning before dawn to study, by candlelight, reports of the sanitary conditions in the London, Paris, and Berlin hospitals. She filled notebooks with statistical information about public health, keeping detailed records of all that she learned.

A 26-year-old Florence wrote, "I feel as if all my being were gradually drawing together to one point." But every attempt to apply her growing knowledge was thwarted by family pressure to act in accordance with their high station in life, so Florence remained at home and continued her studies in secret.

Over the next several years, her torment and sense of worthlessness increased, at times driving her to the verge of madness. She felt that she'd accomplished nothing in life. "Busy idleness" was how she described her life condition.

At age 31, Florence finally managed to break away from her family to take medical training, first at a German institute with religious roots, then in a Paris hospital where the nurses were nuns. She finally took a nursing position in a London hospital. Her desire to nurse was, to her mind, a calling to serve—her mission.

Hospital positions at that time were often secured either through bribery or nepotism. A nurse's qualifications were seldom the primary factor considered at hiring time. Florence fought the system. She became a one woman crusade for better quality nurses and doctors. A skillful negotiator, she made many important contacts among people of prominence, enlisting their support to bring about reforms in the hospital where she worked.

Out of consideration for those of you who have eaten within the past 24 hours, I won't detail the squalid conditions of European hospital wards in the mid-19th Century. Let this example suffice: During the Crimean War, hospitals swelled with the wounded. Imagine one thousand soldiers suffering from diarrhea in a hospital equipped with only 20 chamber pots.

Florence Nightingale served the cause in a Constantinople military hospital, where she faced a seemingly insurmountable task. She had to improve sanitary conditions, train a qualified staff of nurses and doctors, and overcome political corruption and petty jealousies. Accustomed to comfort and luxury, this determined woman lived under the worst conditions imaginable, but she was on a mission. "Resignation...," she once wrote, "I never understood that word."

The hospitalized soldiers adored her. As a show of respect, they even gave up swearing! Those who recuperated and later returned home to their families spoke of her kindness to them. Stories of her sacrifice and caring spread throughout England. Florence Nightingale became a national heroine. Queen Victoria, herself, came to praise her efforts.

During this time, Florence also improved the wounded soldiers' intellectual and spiritual lives, encouraging the men to send money home, better themselves, and give up drinking. She further assisted them to reform their personal behavior by helping to open schools for the soldiers' education. Florence accomplished all of this while suffering a variety of personal health challenges. A slight woman who never enjoyed good health, she endured sciatic pain, recurring earaches, laryngitis, and chronic bouts of insomnia. Despite these physical ailments, she managed, in just a few years, to revolutionize how the public viewed nurses, doctors, and British soldiers.

Seventy-three percent of the deaths during the Crimean War were due to disease. At home after the war, Florence paced her room at night, driven to formulate a plan for the complete overhaul of the Army Medical Department. Once genuine reform of military hospitals was underway, she turned her attention to improving conditions in civil hospitals as well.

Dealing with the inflated egos of bureaucrats was a constant source of frustration, and it took its toll on her health. At one point, she became so ill that the *London Daily News* wrote her obituary in expectation of her imminent demise.

Florence rallied. By age 39, she was an invalid who seldom left her bedroom, and never left the house. Yet she continued to work relentlessly for reform in every aspect of patient care, medical training, and hospital design—even suggesting the most soothing color to paint hospital room walls. She opened a school for aspiring nurses, training them to her own high standards. Next came a school for the training of midwives.

Only 40 years old, she required constant physical care. "I am so much weaker," she wrote, "that I do not sit up at all now." But she wouldn't let her health challenges impede her progress or lessen her administrative efforts.

Through reams of correspondence during our Civil War, she guided the United States War Department with her detailed instructions for hospital reorganization and improved patient care. Later, she became a pioneer of the first Red Cross movement.

Florence Nightingale could have been the poster girl for the elements of success. Her faith, commitment to purpose, and inexhaustible energy to act on her dreams were astounding testimonials to the power of having desire. "I think one's feelings waste themselves in words," she said. "They ought all to be distilled into actions which bring results."

2. The Dumb Kid's Desire Took Him to the Top. Ben Carson grew up in a Detroit ghetto. His father left the family when Ben was only eight, and never returned. The boy's mother, a woman with just a third-grade education, was determined to see Ben succeed in life. "You weren't born to be a failure," she said. "You can do it!"

Poverty forced the family to leave its home and move to a roach and rat-infested tenement. The determined mother eventually managed to reclaim her former home—a house the size of a garage.

Ben, who was black, was the lowest achieving student in his predominately white, fifth-grade class. Kids can be cruel. Ben's classmates teased and made fun of him. He was labeled "the dumb kid," the kid at the bottom of his class.

Mom took action. She curtailed television viewing, pushing Ben to study more and play less. One of her rules was that two library books would be checked out and read each week. Ben Carson's mom believed her son could become the best reader in his class. Her faith in him fostered a faith in himself. Ben liked nature and animals, so he chose to read science books. Although it was drudgery at first, reading soon helped his school grades soar. His vocabulary and comprehension improved. His self-confidence grew. Ben's mother told him he could learn about anything through reading. He began to believe it. His own goal now was to become the smartest kid in class. Ben was filled with the desire to achieve. Self-development excited him.

Within two years, the "dumb" kid had, indeed, become the smartest student in his class. His emphasis then shifted. Being smarter than everyone else was no longer enough. Ben wanted to be the best he could be, so he challenged himself to learn more, do more, and be more. Ben Carson set a new goal for himself. He would become a doctor.

His exceptional academic achievement secured him a scholarship and entry into one of the country's top colleges. Ben attended Yale.

Classes were tough. Surrounded by students brighter than any he'd seen back home, Ben found college a real challenge. He was failing chemistry. Used to cramming for tests in high school, he discovered that this approach to study didn't work at Yale. He faced a thick chemistry book the night before his final exam and knew that he'd fail. Failure meant the end of his dream to become a doctor.

Ben prayed for a miracle that night. Exhausted, he went to sleep, and dreamed he was in the chemistry lecture hall, where the professor was working out a series of problems on the blackboard. Then Ben awoke and quickly wrote down all he could remember from that blackboard in his dream.

The following morning, he took his seat in the chemistry lecture hall, and grew ecstatic when the test questions proved to be the very ones answered in his dream the night before. Ben Carson passed his final exam—with a 97.

Believing that his life had been created for a purpose, Ben decided, then, to dedicate himself to what he called "in-depth" learning. He studied to gain as much knowledge as possible, not simply to get good grades. He devoted himself to acquiring knowledge for the sake of knowledge. He reformed his study habits and immersed himself in all his subjects.

Ben Carson's mom had told him, "Bennie, it doesn't really matter what color you are. If you're good, you'll be recognized. Because people, even if they're prejudiced, are going to want the best. You just have to make being the best your goal in life."

By age 33, Dr. Ben Carson had become head of pediatric neural surgery at Johns Hopkins Hospital. Today, he lives and works with an unshakable faith that each of us is endowed with great potential. We are all blessed with gifts that come out of our desire.

Want to be inspired? Read Ben Carson's autobiography, *Gifted Hands*. This man's desire spawned his gift—extraordinary hand and eye coordination. It took him from a squalid existence in a Detroit ghetto to a rewarding life of healing in medical service to others.

3. Strength in the Tenacity of Having Desire Reveals the Gift. "Blessed is he who carries within himself a God, an ideal, and who obeys it," said scientist Louis Pasteur. "[An] ideal of art, ideal of science, ideal of the gospel virtues, therein lie the springs of great thoughts and actions; they all reflect light from the Infinite." Louis Pasteur's own life exemplified the truth of these words.

In his teens he displayed a strong analytical ability. His mind worked so painstakingly on problems that some teachers thought he was slow. Naturally inquisitive, he immersed himself in his studies. Leisure time was spent at the library, where he liked to read biographies of great men and women. He was hungry to learn and benefit from the experiences of illustrious people.

Pasteur's powers of examination and investigation eventually led him into the field of chemistry. At the time he lived, in the mid-19th Century, scientists saw a great many people fall sick and die from disease. He was determined to understand the workings of microorganisms, and to find ways to prevent the spread of germs.

Pasteur held the "wild theory" that germs were spread by floating through the air, contaminating our food and drink, and causing people to contract a wide variety of deadly diseases. These ideas were considered scientific heresy by many of his peers. The widely accepted belief at the time was that germs were caused by spontaneous generation. That is, they somehow arose from inanimate matter, and scientists were at a loss as to how to stop the process. Pasteur endured much criticism and personal attack from the establishment, who felt their scientific reputations were threatened by his opinions.

Surgical operations 150 years ago were often successful, but patients died anyway. Doctors didn't understand the need to sterilize against germs. No one took precautions that are now routine. Creating an antiseptic environment for patients wasn't even a consideration.

Louis Pasteur's research was instrumental in changing that. He demonstrated the need for sterilization against germs to protect people from infectious diseases. He also pioneered work in the creation of vaccines, giving patients a weakened strain of the germ to stimulate immunity to the disease.

During years of working in conflict with a hostile scientific community, Pasteur dealt with much personal hardship as well. He buried three of his young children and, at age 45, suffered a debilitating stroke which paralyzed his entire left side. The scientist turned to a hope-inducing habit from his youth. He read accounts of famous people who, through their courage and perseverance, overcame failure, illness, and other personal setbacks. Through long months of convalescence, Pasteur focused his mind on returning to work.

"A man's life is useless if not spent in service to others," he said. Three months after the stroke, he was carried back into his laboratory where, from his bed or sofa, he directed his assistants in research and scientific experiments.

Pasteur's dedication to his dream revolutionized the scientific community. His research saved countless lives from being lost to rabies, diphtheria, tuberculosis, and many other diseases. Toward the end of his life, he helped to create the Pasteur Institute, in Paris, where his important work to relieve human suffering could continue.

"Let me tell you the secret that has led me to my goal," Pasteur once said. "My strength lies solely in my tenacity." Not fewer hurdles but more jumps are what is needed.

4. An Illuminating Desire Releases the Genius Within. Inventor Thomas Edison experimented with 2,000 different filaments for his new idea, the electric light, with no success. After 2,000 failed attempts to get that incandescent bulb to stay lit, friends and family began to think he was wasting his time.

I imagine myself in that situation. I'm doing a drawing, and some part of it isn't working. It doesn't look right. So I use another approach; then another. Would I be willing to experiment with 2,000 different approaches to the same challenge? Apply that to your own life. Would you have the patience, discipline, and desire to hang in there that long?

At that point in his experiments, Edison was interviewed by a reporter who asked, "Sir, how does it feel to have failed 2,000 times?" Edison looked at him and said, "Son, I haven't failed. I've succeeded in finding 2,000 filaments that will not work!"

Now *that's* perseverance. Given that mental attitude, Edison couldn't be anything but successful. He said, "Many of life's failures are [created by] people who did not realize how close they were to success when they gave up." Make sure your final attempt is the successful one.

Luck enters only when we hold the door open for it—even after our arm starts to ache. As someone said, "Luck happens when preparation and opportunity meet." You might also think of luck as an acronym for "Labor Under Correct Knowledge." The stronger your desire, the luckier you'll get.

Fail Often and Have Fun with It

British playwright J.M. Barrie wrote, "We are all of us failures—at least, the best of us are." Barrie understood the positive role failure can play in our lives. Edison certainly knew he had one of the greatest failure rates ever. But he considered failure as a powerful learning tool when properly utilized. Today, his name is synonymous with the words "genius" and "success."

Defeat provides the best homework assignments. Failure is always part of the picture. You can't avoid it. Our education consists largely of learning what won't work. Think about it. The more you're willing to fail, the greater your chance for success. Like all great people do, Edison literally failed his way to success. And so can you. Don't be afraid to fail.

While feelings of futility are, at times, inevitable, remember, they're just feelings. They'll pass when we learn to weather them with faith. Successful people awaken to days of dark moods but they get out of bed and get moving anyway. In the final analysis, people who ultimately fail curl into a fetal position and pull the blanket of futility over their heads.

The Japanese have a wonderful proverb: "Fall seven times, stand up eight." Successful people are simply people who formerly failed, have a stubborn, persistent desire, and an undying belief in themselves and the value of what they're doing.

We need to be more like children in our quest to succeed. Kids make mistakes and generally take it in stride. At some level, they understand that it's only a part of their learning. Did you color inside the lines the first time you picked up a crayon? Did you stay upright on your bicycle the day your training wheels came off? Be more childlike in your approach to life. Don't mind falling on your backside now and then. Better to fall on your backside than to just sit on it and not strive to reach your goals and dreams!

The fear of looking foolish is a foolish way to look at yourself. Every face, seen in the right light, has traces of egg on it. Keep a playful perspective on all things, and you'll always have plenty of shelf-space in your medicine cabinet.

Laugh and the world laughs with you. Cry and your mascara runs, or your face gets wet. A sense of humor was given to human beings because we need one. Feel free to cultivate and use it.

"*Some people fail and call it fate.
Themselves they discombobulate.
They sit and sigh. Their dreams
deflate. Success can't come; there's no
debate, to struggle on would just frus-
trate. I may as well capitulate,
I know my place.... I'm second-rate.
Others, when they fall prostrate,
just rise again to illustrate
that faith and will can dominate.
Resiliently such people state,
if failure comes it is not fate,
despair I will eradicate.
These setbacks serve to stimulate,
they cause my brain to innovate.
All doubts and fears evaporate
as confidence I emanate.
Myself I'll never underrate.
Success I do anticipate.*"

—Bruce Garrabrandt

"Motivation is no eternal flame. It needs daily stoking. Your attitude either fuels or smothers the fire."

—Bruce Garrabrandt

The Power of Having Desire

*"...intense desire creates not only its
own opportunities, but also its own talents."*
— Eric Hoffer —

When you sincerely want success—and apply yourself—you can have it. It's easier said than done, of course, but then *everything* is easier said than done. So what? Just go do it!

Take, for example, my father-in-law. He never went beyond the tenth grade. It was during the Depression, and he quit school to find work so he could help his family. After serving in World War II, he came home to a blue collar, factory job. The money wasn't good.

As the years passed, the money never became good, but he still managed to pay off a mortgage and support a family, even though he never liked his job. But while his coworkers met after hours at a local bar to hoist a few and complain about their lot in life, my father-in-law studied books on carpentry, plumbing, and electricity—filling his head with practical knowledge. He had the desire to go into business for himself. The power of having this desire enabled him to cultivate his gifts and talents. It was his gift.

He remembered the day he retired from his factory job. After work, he drop-kicked his lunch pail down the street. For the rest of his life, he had all the business he could handle. His phone was always ringing with jobs to be done. His practical skills, self-taught, kept him in demand—and making good money.

People often ask the question, "How can I get motivated and stay motivated?" To me, that's like asking, "How do I get dressed in the morning? How do I brush my teeth? How do I keep from starving to death?" *You* take responsibility for all these things. No one else but you can give you a sustaining belief in yourself or the ongoing desire to achieve. No one but you can act on that desire. Just like my father-in-law, the power of having desire will enable you to cultivate *your* gifts and talents. It will help you develop the discipline and perseverance needed to reach your dreams and goals.

I'll tell you something that helps many people stay motivated, and it will help you too. Talk to your leader or mentor. Ask for a recommended reading list of positive books. Read from one of them at least 15-20 minutes a day. Great times to do this are during your early morning alone time, at coffee or lunch breaks at work, and right before you turn the light out to go to sleep.

Also, as suggested before, ask your leader or mentor for a list of recommended continuing education audio tapes or CDs. Listen to them as you get ready for the day, while driving in your car, and preparing for bed. Listen to these recordings again and again. People who win are on a constant quest for knowledge and keep themselves motivated.

Shared knowledge of universal truths forms the broadest brotherhood, spaning both space and time. We think of the great men and women of history as having been larger than life, but they were no larger than you and I. They suffered the same doubts, frustrations, and setbacks that we all face, and probably more. We have much to learn from them about life, success, and the power of having desire.

Samuel Johnson, the 18th Century writer, said, "Life, though it be short, is made shorter by waste of time." Based on insurance company actuarial tables, I have only 1,600 weeks left to live. But if the insurance companies are wrong and I see my 100th birthday, I have about 3,000 more weeks to live. That fact helps me stay focused.

Life is a wonderful function to which everyone is invited, but millions have either failed to ask for directions to it or else copied down the wrong address. Don't be one of them.

I truly admire the late Steve Allen. I had an opportunity to meet and speak with him some years ago. He used time more efficiently than anyone else I know. To function well, he unfortunately needed 10 to 12 hours of sleep, but he learned how to maximize his productivity while awake. The author of 53 books, he dictated them into small tape recorders he kept in his pocket, on the nightstand by his bed, and in his car. He was the composer of more than 5,000 songs, which placed him in the *Guinness Book of World Records*. When he wasn't writing jokes, he stayed busy with a full schedule of concert and night-club appearances.

At 78, Steve Allen continued to think creatively and productively. His final performance was given the night before he died—to a sold-out house.

He liked to say, "We should all die with our desks left cluttered with tasks yet to be done." His life was dedicated to the fulfillment of his dreams and desires. These pursuits brought meaning, vitality, and joy to all of his days.

Death is Nature's way of reminding us to get busy. Enjoy but never settle for what and where you are. Always strive to accomplish even bigger dreams. As shared before, success is found in the journey. Being complacent is often an indication that you're not doing enough.

The first step to a successful life is to realize that everything you need for success is already within you—you were born with it. Motivational speakers and authors can and do inspire us, but the only "motivational speaker" who can move *you* into action is *you*. So speak your desire to *yourself* and get moving. That's where you'll find your power.

What do you most desire in life? That is your gift. Act on it with faith, discipline, and perseverance and, in time, you will be successful. If I can do it with art, you can achieve your dream, too, in whatever area of endeavor you may choose. Commit to developing your potential capabilities today, take action, and watch your unique talents emerge. Discover the power of having desire.

"What is your gift? Take that gift—which is your passion or desire—and commit to making it happen. Act on it with relentless discipline and perseverance, and you will be successful."

—Bruce Garrabrandt

"**Y**our best opportunity is *NOW*."

—Bruce Garrabrandt

Who Is Bruce Garrabrandt?

Bruce Garrabrandt is a popular and sought after professional artist, writer, and inspiring motivational speaker. With his wife, Jan, he is also innkeeper of *The Artist's Inn & Gallery*, a bed and breakfast nestled in the heart of Pennsylvania Dutch Country.